C0061 70169

D0248256

**Amanda Gummer** is a research psychologist specialising in child development. She has over 20 years' experience working with children and families, including lecturing for The Open University on child development and teaching children with special needs in Hong Kong. She is the resident psychologist and a co-founder of Karisma Kidz, a non-executive director for Families in Focus CIC and the resident psychologist for UKMums.TV. She also provides consultancy and training on issues facing parents to a wide range of audiences.

Widely considered as *the* go-to expert on play, toys and child development, Amanda is regularly in the media, and continues to take an active role in research, presenting a paper at the International Toy Research Association's World Congress in Portugal in July. She is often involved in government policy around children's issues, having recently contributed to the Bailey Review and the Good Childhood Inquiry.

Amanda heads up Fundamentally Children, providers of the popular parenting advice site www.fundamentallychildren.com, home of the Good Toy Guide and Good App Guide, so is surrounded by play on a daily basis as she observes children engaging with the latest toys and apps. She has two children of her own and so understands how much more enjoyable a playful family life can be.

# Fun ways to help your child develop in the first five years

## DR AMANDA GUMMER

**Vermilion**
LONDON

1 3 5 7 9 10 8 6 4 2

Vermilion, an imprint of Ebury Publishing,
20 Vauxhall Bridge Road,
London SW1V 2SA

Vermilion is part of the Penguin Random House group of companies
whose addresses can be found at global.penguinrandomhouse.com

Penguin
Random House
UK

Copyright © Dr Amanda Gummer 2015
Illustration copyright © 2015 Stephanie Strickland

Dr Amanda Gummer has asserted her right to be identified as the author of this
Work in accordance with the Copyright, Designs and Patents Act 1988

First published by Vermilion in 2015

www.eburypublishing.co.uk

A CIP catalogue record for this book is available from the British Library

ISBN 9780091955144

Printed and bound in Great Britain by Clays Ltd, St Ives PLC

Penguin Random House is committed to a sustainable future for our business, our readers
and our planet. This book is made from Forest Stewardship Council® certified paper.

MIX
Paper from
responsible sources
FSC® C018179

The information in this book has been compiled by way of general guidance in
relation to the specific subjects addressed, but is not a substitute and not to be relied
on for medical, healthcare, pharmaceutical or other professional advice on specific
circumstances and in specific locations. So far as the author is aware the information
given is correct and up to date as at January 2015. Practice, laws and regulations all
change, and the reader should obtain up to date professional advice on any such issues.
The author and publishers disclaim, as far as the law allows, any liability arising directly
or indirectly from the use, or misuse, of the information contained in this book.

*This book is dedicated to my parents with thanks for a fun-filled*
*childhood, in memory of Nan and Dood, who were always up*
*for a game (the sillier the better), and for my gorgeous girls*
*Katie and Frankie – may you never feel too old to play.*

| Glasgow Life Glasgow Libraries | |
|---|---|
| GH | |
| C 006170169 | |
| Askews & Holts | 08-Jun-2016 |
| 649.5   FH | £10.99 |
| | |

WITHDRAWN

# Contents

# Introduction

The first few months and even years of parenthood can feel like boot camp – with the lack of sleep, physical exhaustion and no sense of it ever ending. I have written this book to support you in not only surviving but also thriving as a parent, allowing you to help your child develop through play, be a wonderful role model for your child and have plenty of fun along the way. By giving you practical tips, no-nonsense advice and plenty of opportunities to share laughter with your children, I hope you feel more confident, relaxed and able to balance the needs of your whole family.

As we are all individuals, with different family circumstances, demands and resources, it is important that you read this book through the lens of your own family life. Consider your personal values, your challenges and your aspirations, and make it part of your unique journey into parenthood. There is no generic, one-size-fits-all manual for babies and children, instead this book allows you to start compiling your own personal guide for your child. There is plenty of space at the end of each chapter to write your own comments on what has worked and what has not. Use it to record the developmental features and milestones that your baby achieves – it might even come in useful for the next one!

Playing with your child doesn't have to come with a high price tag. There are plenty of ways in which you can promote healthy child development through play on a low budget and, in many cases, for free. In each chapter, I have suggested playful activities and explained what skills those activities develop.

This book is a practical and light-hearted alternative to all those 'how-to' parenting guides. Have fun trying out some of the activities and enjoy putting play into your daily family life.

## Play: Frivolous Fun or Serious Learning?

The benefits of play are often discounted by adults who want children to 'do it properly' and 'stop messing about', but children are programmed to play – it's how they learn best.

The Department for Education advocates learning through play in the early years foundation stage of the national curriculum (ages one to five), and the leading preschools and nurseries also promote play, especially child-led play, as the most effective way of teaching children important skills.

Building blocks, arts and crafts, role play, water or sand and a range of other play activities and toys can encourage your child's natural curiosity in safe, age-appropriate ways. Parents are often surprised at what their children learn when given the freedom to play their way, without the usual constraints of adults' rules and directions.

Trial and error is a key feature of children's free play. It is a powerful tool for enhancing your child's understanding of the world, as she explores: 'I wonder what happens if ...' Children can be engrossed in activities that are as important to them as controlled scientific experiments are to scientists.

However, learning based purely on trial and error is very inefficient, as it does not take advantage of lessons learned by other people's experiences. If a child is left to develop purely by trial and error, she will end up making a plethora of mistakes, some of which can be dangerous or even life-threatening (e.g. 'I wonder what happens if I walk across a road with my eyes shut …'). We have spent millions of years evolving, learning and improving things. Your child can benefit from your experience and knowledge, and if you give her plenty of opportunities to play it will equip her with the skills and motivation to add her own contribution to the world too.

You can help your child learn safely by 'scaffolding' her. This provides her with the guidance that prevents dangerous mistakes and enhances her chances of success, but that still enables her to try things out for herself.

Doing everything for your child may be quicker in the short term, but learning through personal experience is the most long-lasting and so it is important that she is allowed to try things out (and occasionally fail) in order to benefit from the learning opportunities play affords.

Next time your child floods the bathroom or squeezes a bottle of ketchup with its lid off, don't worry, she is learning – even if part of the lesson she learns is that what she has done has made Mummy cross; it is all part of growing up.

In the past, little thought was given to the importance of play and how it contributed to the developing child, so it is natural that some parents see it as merely a fun activity, a reward or even a waste of time. However, incorporating fun themes into children's learning from an early stage makes the experience more memorable for them and less daunting so that they will feel more positive towards it.

Think back to your own childhood:

- What do you remember from school?
- What were the most valuable lessons you ever learnt?
- What was the most effective way for you to learn and retain information?
- When did you most enjoy learning?
- What was your favourite toy?

Reminding yourself of your own childhood is often a good check and balance for your own parenting. Are there certain activities that you enjoyed as a child, or is there something your parents did that you wouldn't want to repeat? Recreating some of those things you most enjoyed will help you bond with your baby and rediscover your inner child. You will probably also remember how much fun you had when you were free to play naturally (we all did much more of it in those days) – this will help you resist pressures to hothouse or overschedule your child.

It is important to note that there is a difference between *helping* a child to learn and *pushing* a child to learn. Children who are pressured early on do not fare any better than those who are allowed to take their time; children learn best through simple playtime, which enhances problem-solving skills, attention span, social development and creativity. The recent increase in anxiety and mental health issues in children may be due to the pressures faced by young children who are not given the freedom and opportunity to play.

Free play also allows children to develop the important skill of independent thinking. If you embrace play as part of your child's development it will give her a greater incentive to learn through her natural curiosity.

## How This Book Works

This book is a progression through the first five years of your child's life, split into chapters based on age. Each chapter focuses on a key aspect of development that is particularly relevant for children around that age.

As well as outlining key developmental features within each stage, the chapters are full of practical ideas for play and advice on how to promote your child's development with fun activities. There are also useful sections about the types of toys that children at each stage are likely to engage with to help you manage birthdays and Christmases, and to avoid toys that will just end up in the back of the cupboard or be five-minute wonders. For some further play ideas you can also visit www.fundamentallychildren.com.

Please try not to get too hung up on the ages: look more at the skills that come next for your child based on where she is at any point in time. Use the advice and playful activities to encourage development of the next skill, but don't hothouse or worry if she seems to be lagging behind in some areas – children don't develop uniformly. Make sure you manage your expectations, taking into account factors such as prematurity and illness when assessing whether your child is thriving, and try not to be overly anxious if she seems to be slower at achieving some milestones than her peers, or if her pattern of development seems to span more than one chapter.

Towards the end of each chapter there is a troubleshooting section, 'It Is Not Always Easy', which provides practical advice on resolving common issues that may have been causing you frustration or anxiety. At the end of the book (pages 203–8), there is also a list of useful resources for additional information on topics covered in this book, as well as signposts to specialist advice on issues raised.

At the end of each chapter I have added 10 fun things that you can try to do at some point in her childhood. Tick them off as and when they are achieved, and feel free to add more as you go … You can keep these lists as a memory – and you can do them all over again with your grandchildren.

## Genetic conditions and additional needs

All babies are special and unique and come with their own set of challenges. One of the biggest challenges for new parents is finding out that your baby has a genetic condition resulting in physical or cognitive impairments.

The advice in this book is relevant to *all* parents. Children with genetic conditions, such as Down's syndrome, may develop the skills in the book more slowly than the age grouping in the chapters suggest, but they will still develop the skills in approximately the same order and still deserve to have a playful childhood.

Children with specific physical impairments, such as deafness, blindness or limb deformity, will develop additional skills in other areas to compensate for their specific impairment, and, hopefully, you will still find lots of the book very relevant and useful, though some of the play ideas will not be appropriate. Try thinking of other activities that achieve a similar aim.

My advice to all parents is to celebrate the things your baby can do and help her develop coping strategies for things that she finds challenging.

If you are worried about your child's development, do seek advice. Most problems are more easily treated if diagnosed early. Talk to friends and family, especially those with children a little older than yours, but don't be afraid to seek professional help either. The best place to seek advice for non-emergency issues is at your local children's centre – the health visitors there will be able to help you determine whether there is an underlying medical issue and, if so, where best to go for more specialist help. You can also discuss any concerns with your GP.

I really hope you find the practical advice in the following pages useful and that my play ideas will promote a fun childhood, while also supporting holistic development. Please remember that all children progress at different rates and my suggestions are just guides. The best piece of advice I can give you is to enjoy your child and have as much fun with her as possible, laying down memories and behavioural patterns that will serve her well in later life and make your whole family closer.

**Please note that throughout the book I have referred to all children as 'she' purely for ease and consistency.**

# Chapter One
# Playful Beginnings
# (0–2 Months)

The first few weeks of a baby's life are a period of adjustment for both parents and babies, and are rarely without challenges. Overcoming these challenges and maintaining a positive, playful approach to family life can promote attachment, enhance involvement and acceptance of the new baby by other family members, as well as help avoid postnatal depression. However, it can be a tall order to maintain an optimistic, playful attitude when you're faced with broken sleep, a fractious baby and the hormonal turmoil that accompanies the very first few weeks of parenthood.

It is important for your baby that you are able to look after yourself in these early weeks. If you are feeling healthy and calm, you will be more able to identify and respond appropriately to your baby's different cries and more equipped to cope with broken sleep. You will also feel more inclined and motivated to continue to nurture the relationships that are important to you, thus providing a healthy role model for your baby to copy and learn from, and providing you with a valuable support network.

New babies can seem very passive and, as new parents get to grips with an addition to the family, it is easy to miss some of the more subtle signs of development associated with the first few weeks of life. The most noticeable development at this age is physical: regaining birth weight and strengthening muscles. However, important foundations are also being laid for cognitive, emotional and social development from the day your baby is born.

Babies can hear noises inside the womb, and hearing matures quickly after birth. Taste and smell is fully developed when your baby is born, whereas vision takes a few more weeks to fully mature. Your baby will be hypersensitive to touch due to the concentration of nerve receptors over her small body, but she won't yet be able to coordinate her movements or use touch to explore the world in the same way an adult does. A baby will use her lips and tongue to learn about shape, texture and temperature, as well as the taste of objects in her world.

This chapter will identify some of the main milestones to watch out for and suggest playful ways for you to encourage healthy development.

## What to Look Out for During this Stage

All babies develop differently, and premature babies need to be given time to catch up developmentally with their peers. When charting a premature baby's development make sure you take into account her corrected age (the original due date), as she will take months, if not a couple of years, to 'catch up'.

The following key features of development are ones that you will enjoy noticing during the first few weeks of your baby's life.

## Physical and sensory development

### Vision

Young babies will focus on contrasting colours. Your baby may stare at edges of pictures, windows or images with contrasting colours. Her vision will mature rapidly over the first few weeks of life, allowing her to focus on increasingly more detailed or subtle images and objects.

Babies, even newborns, are predisposed to looking at faces – a trait that enables them to quickly recognise their primary carer's face, thus promoting bonding and attachment. She will start to recognise faces within two weeks.

### Hearing

Hearing sudden noises and turning towards them is something babies do from an early age. All babies should be given a hearing test within the first few weeks of their life (if you haven't had this, contact your health visitor); however, you can also encourage listening skills, and check her hearing ability, by laying your baby on her back and making a loud noise to one side of her, in her line of vision. If she hears it, she should roll her head towards the sound. Early detection of hearing problems can help prevent speech delays, so it is a good idea to regularly play games with your baby that involve sound. She will be able to recognise her parents' voices within two weeks.

### Head control

It is important to support a newborn baby's head until she can support it on her own (normally after at least five weeks). Her neck muscles can be strengthened by holding her to your chest, so that she can look over your shoulder and start to lift her head, but make sure you are able to support it if she suddenly lurches backwards.

## 'Tummy time'

Your baby spends a large amount of time on her back sleeping, but she also requires time on her front to develop both physically and mentally. This is known as 'tummy time', and it is great for encouraging babies to lift up their heads to develop their neck muscles. Try moving around the room while your baby is lying on her tummy to motivate her to try to lift her head, as she will want to watch you.

## Reflexes

Babies are born with automatic reflexes and these are key indicators that their nervous system is 'wired' correctly. For example, if a bright light is shone in your baby's face she will close her eyes, if something is put in her mouth she will automatically suck on it and if something is put in her hands she will close her fist around it and hold on tightly enough to be able to support her own weight. Many of the reflexes disappear after a few months, but it's good to check that they are there in the first few weeks and talk to your health visitor if you have any concerns.

### Root reflex

This is the reflex that helps a newborn find her mother's breast to feed. You can test this reflex with a gentle stroke on her cheek – your baby should turn towards your touch, with an open mouth, ready to nurse.

The root reflex will start to fade when your baby is between three and four months old (although some babies continue doing this in their sleep past four months). As the reflex disappears, babies increasingly use their sense of smell, sight and hearing to predict when food is coming. The rooting reflex can often be misunderstood as a sign of hunger, but your baby will root whenever something touches her cheek, regardless of how hungry she is.

### Sucking reflex

This is one of the most important reflexes your child is born with as it enables her to feed. Her sucking reflex is triggered when something (such as a nipple, teat or parent's finger) touches the roof of her mouth. She will respond by sucking on the nipple or teat, which in turn will enable her to get milk.

She will lose this reflex at around four months old, by which time your baby has learnt to recognise the breast or bottle and starts sucking in anticipation.

As the sucking reflex isn't fully developed until around 36 weeks of pregnancy, premature babies will need to be tube fed until they acquire this reflex. All premature babies will develop at different rates; this could be earlier or later than others, particularly depending on how premature she is. Introducing a soother can encourage the sucking reflex.

### *Grasp reflex (or palmar grasp reflex)*

Your baby's grasp reflex is present up until she is about four months old and can be tested by gently pressing a finger, or other suitable object, into your baby's palm. Her grasp can be incredibly strong and she can even pull herself up when gripping with both hands.

### *Startle reflex (or Moro reflex)*

You may have noticed your baby jump occasionally when she hears or senses a loud noise or sudden movement from the person who is holding her. She may even startle when experiencing a sensation of falling. She may cry when this happens, but more often than not she will simply extend and retract her arms and legs very quickly. This reflex should disappear between four and six months old.

### *Babinski reflex*

When you firmly stroke the sole of your baby's foot, her toes will flare out and her big toes point upwards. Once her nervous system is more developed this reflex should disappear. However, it's not uncommon for it to stay until 24 months.

### Stepping/dance reflex

While holding your baby upright (supporting her head) with her feet on a flat surface, she will start to make walking movements with her legs, lifting one foot, then the other. She will continue to do this for about eight weeks after birth.

### Tonic neck reflex (or fencing reflex)

When you lay your one-month-old baby on her back with her head turned to one side, the arm on that side extends while her other arm bends at the elbow, creating a 'fencing' position. She will keep this reflex until she is about six months old. This reflex is believed to aid passage through the birth canal.

## Thinking and communication

Babies communicate from the moment they are born. Crying is the most primitive form of communication, but you will notice other signs and movements in your baby that you will soon learn to know as hunger (excessive rooting – see above), wind (arching her back) and tiredness (yawning). At this age babies have no control over the communication signals that they are giving off, but parents' responses to them will lay the foundations for voluntary communication in the future.

### Smiling

It is easy to confuse the expression a baby makes when releasing wind with a smile, but at around four to six weeks many babies will smile in response to a pleasant stimulus. Make sure you smile a lot at your baby, especially when you notice her looking at you, and ensure it's genuine! (Children are better than adults at reading non-verbal communication cues, as they pay attention to all parts of your face and body, so a fake, 'mouth only' smile will confuse a baby.)

## Social and emotional development

You may have already heard of the 'Mozart effect' – the developmental benefits reportedly observed in children who listened to classical music as babies. However, further research[1] has found that it's not only classical music that is beneficial for babies: the 'Mozart effect' has been observed with any music with a strong rhythm and repeating pattern. The precise explanation of the effect is not yet clear, but it is correlated with language and mathematical ability in older children.

An additional effect of music is that it can help calm and regulate a baby's heartbeat. A newborn's resting heart rate is normally around 120–180 beats per minute, reducing significantly during the first few weeks of life to around 80–140 beats per minute. If the rhythm of the music is more than a few beats per minute faster or slower than the baby's heart rate, not much will happen, but if it is close to the heart rate, the baby's heartbeat may align itself with the beat of the music. If the beat of the music is gradually reduced, the baby's heartbeat will mirror it, thus calming an excited baby and aiding sleep (see 'musical magic' on page 23 for more information).

Music can also be used to cover other noises that can disturb a baby and prevent sleep. Sudden noises, such as doors banging and phones ringing, can stimulate a baby and startle her out of restful sleep. When your baby is going to sleep, try having simple music on in the background to mask other noises and enable her to relax and drift off naturally. White noise and audiobooks can produce the same effect (although you should always make sure you can hear your baby's cries over any music or noise).

## Helping an older child accept a new baby

Just like there is no such thing as a 'normal child', there is no 'normal behaviour' for an older child accepting a new baby, and each sibling relationship will be unique. It is common for children to become clingy when a new baby appears on the scene, but they also may reject their mother and transfer affections to another role model such as a grandfather or even childminder. Depending on the age of the child, some may suddenly seem to grow up and enjoy being the big brother or sister, while other children may regress and want babying a bit more.

It is not uncommon for a potty-trained child to start having accidents, need to be fed by an adult or refuse to get dressed like she did before. All these signs are indications that your elder child wants to retain the amount of your attention she had before your newborn arrived. If her behaviour becomes persistent and difficult to manage, try to encourage her to show the new baby what a 'big girl' she is now by feeding herself, going to the toilet on the potty or getting herself dressed. As she becomes more confident that you still love her, still pay her enough attention and she starts to get used to having to share you, this attention-seeking behaviour should start to subside.

### *Typical jealous behaviour an older child may exhibit*
Taking the baby's dummy or toys is common, as is crying about things she would not normally have been bothered

by – attention-seeking behaviour in general is quite common. It can get more extreme and older siblings can intentionally try to hurt the new baby, though this is rare and normally only happens with older children (under-threes won't have the necessary cognitive skills to deliberately hurt the baby, but you should still be wary of experimental accidents).

### How to make your older child still feel special

Make sure your older child feels valued and reassured that you are, and will continue to be, as interested in her as before.

Talk to your toddler and involve her in decisions, for example asking her, 'Do you think the baby would like to wear the blue or the red top today?' Encourage her to help find clothes when getting the baby dressed or pass you the cream when you change the nappy. She will love to be involved and help care for her new sibling, and you can give both children your attention at the same time.

A new baby doll for your child can help her feel more involved and grown up; she can feed her dolly while you feed the new baby and bathe the dolly while you bathe the new baby. Using dolls and role play in this way is a common approach that can work very well, especially with children aged between two and five. Older children can be encouraged to play with the new baby too, and should be given free access to the baby's toys. Siblings can also benefit from revisiting play patterns, which they may have grown out of, and it also provides additional stimulation for the new baby.

It is good to plan exciting things for your child to do with or without you so that your older child has plenty of positive experiences to associate with this period in her life and reduce the chance of resentment of the baby. However, don't undervalue the importance of a cuddle on the sofa with your older child. Where possible, make sure you keep special 'big girl'/'big boy' time where you spend some one-to-one time together. Often it is best to plan this for when the baby is asleep or when there is someone else to look after the baby. Don't be afraid to leave a baby crying for a few minutes to preserve this special time with your older child – it will really help reduce any feelings of jealousy she might have.

### How to help your toddler bond with your new baby
It is best to try to promote bonding as a family. The children will develop their own relationship and, while you can tell the toddler how much the baby loves her and how much the baby watches her, etc., it is better to have family cuddles and show both children that you love them and are able to give them both the love and attention they need. This reduces competitiveness and resentment between the children, which in turn promotes sibling bonding. Children under the age of two will not have any memories of life before the new baby was born so resentment will not be an issue in the long term, but it is good to make sure they are not getting any

unintentionally negative messages about their place in the family.

One of the best things that can happen when you bring a new baby home is that your toddler is fairly indifferent to the baby and is more interested in having fun with other family members. This gives you some time to bond with your new baby and recover from the birth without needing to worry about your older child. So don't worry if your toddler isn't particularly interested in the new baby; they will be big parts of each other's lives for at least the next few decades, so a slow start isn't necessarily a bad thing.

## Playful Activities

Play is not a priority at this age, and certainly babies don't initiate it, but being playful with your baby encourages early smiles and social skills, such as eye contact and attachment. Babies respond to smiles and learn to smile themselves, and this experience as well as the expression of pleasure are the foundations of emotional well-being. The options for playful activities grow quickly over the next few stages, but it's a good idea to adopt a playful approach right from the early days and encourage other children to 'play' with and near the baby too.

It is important not to overstimulate your baby at this early stage; she will not require long periods of entertainment and will soon show signs of having had enough by arching her back, crying or fussing. Keep playful activities to a maximum of five minutes at a time.

These are a few activities you can use to engage with your baby in order to help her understand her new world and environment.

## Mirror, mirror

Holding your baby up to look in a mirror, or holding a baby-safe, unbreakable mirror over her while she lies on her back, will help her recognise herself and you. Practise making different, exaggerated, comical expressions and see how your baby responds. Always try to look your baby in the eye, especially when smiling.

## Peekaboo

To play this, you just need to cover your face with your hands (so your child can't see you), hold it for three seconds, then quickly pull your hands away, saying, 'peekaboo!' Do this again and again. You can hide your face for different lengths of time or hide round a corner or behind a high chair and pop out saying, 'peekaboo'.

You may feel self-conscious playing games such as peekaboo when you're the only one actually 'playing', but the earlier you do play these sorts of games, the quicker your baby will respond and then join in. So get over the embarrassment and play away – you might even rediscover your inner child!

## Funny faces

Smiling at your baby encourages her to smile back. More powerfully, mirroring her back when she smiles at you offers her positive feedback to her actions. Reactions such as this help babies form attachments and reinforce positive behaviour. Smiling releases endorphins in the brain that counteract stress, encouraging your baby to be calmer and more relaxed. And contented babies attract more attention from others and so have more incentives to smile, releasing even more endorphins, and so it continues.

Exaggerating facial expressions and making silly faces reinforces the bond you have and helps your baby recognise your face even more quickly.

### Be a chatterbox

Talk to your baby as much as possible and, although she cannot respond, she will start to become familiar with voices. Hold your baby close to you when speaking to her, with her face about 60 cm (24 inches) away, allowing eye contact to develop; this promotes attachment and provides important building blocks used for developing communication skills.

### 'Round and Round the Garden'

The palm of a newborn baby is quite sensitive and lightly touching her palm with your finger will stimulate this sensitivity. As you say the verse 'Round and Round the Garden' (see page 197 for the full words), gently move your finger around her hand, and as you walk your fingers gently up her arm she will become increasingly aware of different sensations and may tense or relax depending on her awareness. Either action will strengthen her muscles.

### 'This Little Piggy'

This is another tactile game using traditional verse, but with the feet this time. Again, this will stimulate her sense of touch. Start by wiggling her big toe for the 'first piggy' and work your way through to her little toe, saying the 'This Little Piggy' rhyme (see page 197 for the full verse). When you get to her final toe, tickle her leg up to her tummy.

## Blowing raspberries

Gently blowing soft raspberries on your baby's skin during nappy changing or bathing provides her with more sensations and may distract her if she is feeling insecure without clothes or swaddling.

## Shaking your hair

Try shaking your head allowing your hair to sway about and gently tickle your baby's body. The movement of your hair and head will strengthen her eye muscles and ability to focus.

## Musical magic

If you want to calm down your overexcited or fractious baby, start with fast-paced, upbeat music and then gradually slow the music beat down. As mentioned on page 16, the baby's heartbeat will follow suit, relaxing and calming her.

Don't feel that you have to play baby music and lullabies all the time. Put your favourite tunes on and have a gentle dance with your baby – the swinging and swaying movements will move the fluid in her inner ear around, promoting balance and coordination. Dancing may not come naturally to all parents but don't be put off doing this just because you may feel self-conscious. Relax knowing you are in the company of someone who isn't judging your dancing!

## Choosing Toys

Newborn babies are unable to 'play' with toys in the usual sense. They have insufficient hand–eye coordination to deliberately pick up objects, though they will grasp things that are put in their hands, such as rattles and other baby toys. However, they will quickly drop them again, which can be frustrating for their carers as they will be perpetually picking up baby toys (remember, a baby doesn't have the thought processes at this age to notice that she has dropped something so won't look for it or be able to pick it up again).

During the first few weeks of life, your baby's vision is still developing and she will tend to look for longer periods at contrasting colours, like black and white or yellow, rather than the more traditional pastel 'baby' colours. You may want to buy some toys, artwork or books with contrasting colours to look at with your baby and help her vision to develop. Softer colours do, however, have a calming effect, and so pastel-coloured cuddly toys used to comfort a baby are better than bright colours, which are more appropriate for playtime toys.

### Do newborn babies really need any toys?

Rattles, baby gyms and mobiles are a few of the baby toys that are often bought by, or for, expectant parents. The market is flooded with baby toys that claim to promote development, but are these claims justified and what toys, if any, do newborn babies really need?

The answer is that babies don't actually need many toys but some toys are beneficial to their development. What is more important is to provide a stimulating environment for your baby with lots going on – toys can form an important part of this and will promote healthy development.

It is important, however, not to overstimulate a baby with lots of fast-moving images (e.g. television), and they will need quiet rest time to allow their brains to organise and make sense of their new experiences and sensations.

One valid viewpoint is that toys aren't actually for the new baby to play with, but to encourage playfulness around the baby. Whether babies play with toys or not, the presence of toys can increase other people's engagement with an infant. Someone shaking a rattle for her or cuddling a soft toy will provide additional stimuli for the baby and promote social development and attachment. Therefore, toys for very young babies may be less important for the baby directly, but act more as a tool for others to be playful and interactive with her.

## It Is Not Always Easy – Troubleshooting Tips

### 'I feel overwhelmed and emotional'

Once the adrenaline and endorphins have worn off (usually seven to ten days after birth), new mothers can feel overwhelmed with emotions – this is often referred to as the 'baby blues'. Sleep deprivation is starting to kick in at this stage, often coinciding with when the visitors who all flocked to see the new baby and provided help and conversation start to dwindle, and your partner may also return to work. Suddenly it is just you and your baby, and life feels very different to anything you have known before. This can cause a significant loss of confidence and make mums feel anything but playful. A baby's basic needs – warmth, nourishment, comfort and safety – are a parent's responsibility, and this sense of responsibility can feel overwhelming at first. Rest assured that there are strategies for making this less daunting and thus reducing the chances of postnatal depression, resentment and a raft of other feelings that you may not be happy to experience.

It is not unusual for new mothers, especially those who have had a career and active social life before having children, to feel somewhat blindsided by motherhood. How you deal with this can have lasting implications for your family life, so treat yourself kindly and ask for (and accept!) help when offered or needed. Remember, babies don't come with manuals – while books such as this are useful as a resource, they won't tell you what to do at 3am when your baby's just been sick on your fresh sheets.

Feeling out of control is one of the most common emotions that new mothers report, and it can be difficult to get the balance between being available for your baby, looking after yourself and continuing to meet your existing commitments, including housework and domestic chores. If your washing has a tendency to mount up, sing loudly so your baby can hear you as you put the washing on or as you iron to let her know you are around. This promotes bonding while giving you strategies to regain control of your environment. Tidying up with her in a sling close to you is great, as is allowing her to lie in her crib and hear your movements and the vacuum cleaner. In your womb she was surrounded by noises so a silent environment is not essential. Talk and sing to her, touch her skin as you move about, kiss her often and smile at her. She will get warmth, comfort and security from all of these things. Then, when your tasks are done, take some time to play with her, cuddle her and enjoy this amazing time growing together and understanding each other.

Try to remember the person you were before you had children – what made you happy, what made you laugh – and make sure you include some of those activities in your weekly, if not daily, schedule. The long-term benefits of having an emotionally healthy parent are huge, so don't beat yourself up if things don't seem to be going to plan – figure out what is really important to you, what you really need to get done during the day, and try not to worry about the smaller issues.

Time away from your baby can be difficult if you are breastfeeding regularly, and obviously you have to decide what is best for you and your baby. Inviting friends around or visiting them in places where you feel comfortable breastfeeding your baby are the most obvious solutions. In addition, you can try expressing your milk and let a partner or grandparent cover a feed or two. The NHS advises that breast milk can be stored in a sterilised container in the fridge for five days, or up to six months in a freezer. Grandparents and dads can love doing these feeds – they can help them feel involved in something they usually can't offer.

---

## Tips for coping with lack of sleep

No matter how many people warn you about the lack of sleep you are going to receive once your baby has arrived, you can never quite comprehend how tough it is until you experience it for yourself. Here are some tips to help you cope.

- Utilise the time your baby is asleep by resting yourself and if possible have a sleep too. It can be tempting to finish household chores but they can wait – sleep is far more important than washing up at this stage.
- For you to stay in control it is crucial to take care of your mind and body as well as you can. Fresh air is really beneficial to both you and your newborn baby.

The calming effect of walking and fresh air will help your mind, provide you with some physical exercise and can offer social interaction. No matter what time of year it is, get yourself outside and walk (wrapping yourself and baby up if cold and shielding her from the sun if hot). Try taking your baby out in between sleep periods. Allow her to look around, take in her new environment and interact with you and people you meet. The air and sensory stimulation will have a tiring effect on her while making her hungry, and after a good feed she will be more likely to enjoy a deeper and longer sleep.

- Bedtime routines are important to aid your baby's sleep patterns. Create a bedtime routine as early on as possible. A warm bath, with soothing music in the background and dim lighting, can help to relax you and your baby. Follow this with a cuddle in a towel to dry and get her dressed for bed in a calm environment. Her final feed of the day should be a quiet one in a dimly lit room to add to the relaxation. Once she has a bedtime routine, try to stick to it and you will find this time of day an increasingly pleasurable experience.

## 'My baby doesn't seem to hear me'

Every baby will be given a hearing test either in hospital after birth or within a couple of weeks at a clinic. If your baby doesn't receive a hearing test early on, check with your health visitor and find out how you can receive one.

It is also important that your baby shows signs of hearing in her everyday environment. Signs to look for include a startled jump in response to a loud noise, her starting to gurgle or make her own noises by two months or turning her head or making sounds when she hears familiar noises.

You can test your child's hearing through play by doing the following:

- When your baby is starting to fret, start singing to her. Your familiar voice along with the rhythm of song should help to settle her, even if just for a moment or two.
- When she is lying on the floor shake a rattle to one side of her head – she should turn her head to face the source of the noise.

### 'My baby can't support her head'

Your baby will need you to support her head for at least the first month of her life; however, towards two months she should be able to support it by herself. If by three months she is still not able to support her head even slightly it is important to speak to your health visitor.

To help your child build neck muscles through play, place your baby on her back or tummy and make noises on either side of her, encouraging her to turn her head towards the noise.

## 10 Fun Things to Do with Your Child

1. Lie outside on a blanket.
2. Blow raspberries on her tummy.

3. Share a bath together.

4. Walk in the park.

5. Listen to her favourite songs.

6. Sing her a lullaby.

7. Meet up with other babies.

8. Attend a local mother-and-baby group.

9. Give her a baby massage.

10. Visit a local children's centre.

## Making Memories

What is your favourite memory from the first few weeks with your baby?

..............................................................................................

..............................................................................................

Which of the reflexes have you noticed?

..............................................................................................

..............................................................................................

..............................................................................................

What things did you worry about in the first few days that are now no longer a concern?

..............................................................................................

..............................................................................................

..............................................................................................

What would you like to remember to tell other new parents?

..............................................................................................

..............................................................................................

What is the worst bit of advice you've received?

..............................................................................................

..............................................................................................

Which songs do you sing to your child?

..............................................................................................

..............................................................................................

What sort of music settles your baby most effectively?

..............................................................................................

..............................................................................................

Are there any areas of development that you're worried about?

..............................................................................................

..............................................................................................

What happened on your first trip out with your baby? Where did you go? Who with?

..............................................................................................

..............................................................................................

..............................................................................................

..............................................................................................

**play**

## Your Notes

..................................................................................
..................................................................................
..................................................................................
..................................................................................
..................................................................................
..................................................................................
..................................................................................
..................................................................................
..................................................................................
..................................................................................
..................................................................................
..................................................................................
..................................................................................
..................................................................................
..................................................................................
..................................................................................
..................................................................................

# Chapter Two
# Sensory Awakenings
# (2–6 Months)

For the first few weeks babies can seem very passive and oblivious to their surroundings, but it's not long before they start to really 'wake up' to the world. Your baby's world expands as she learns to roll over, sit up, view her surroundings and interact more. She will still spend a lot of time lying flat, but as her head control improves she will be able to spend more time looking at the world from a more upright perspective – perhaps in her baby bouncer or in your arms. This increases opportunities for stimulation and interaction with others, as your baby will be able to see in different directions and can see things further away.

This phase of development is wonderfully rewarding for new parents, but it is not without its challenges. Sleep deprivation and the implications of a new addition to the family are starting to become apparent. As with all change, there are positives and negatives – the trick is to find ways to minimise the negative aspects and maximise the positives. Feeling confident about your role as a parent and understanding how to promote healthy development is one key way of maximising enjoyment of your new role.

This chapter explores your baby's rapidly developing senses and explains how getting into good, playful habits early can pay dividends later.

## What to Look Out for During this Stage

### Physical and sensory development

#### *Vision*

From around two months your baby will notice and be able to track moving objects.

She will still look more at faces and face shapes than at other objects, and big eyes are particularly appealing. While she was able to distinguish contrasting colours within the first few days of life, colour vision will now be developing. By two months bright colours are appealing too and can encourage a baby to focus on an image or object for prolonged periods of time. Colour vision typically develops fully between four and six months.

#### *Hearing*

Your baby will be able to recognise your voice and is more likely to turn towards you when she hears it than when she hears the voices of other adults. Keep talking to her to ensure she develops her language skills (see page 36).

#### *Touch and taste*

Babies will put anything they can into their mouths and will use the millions of nerve endings concentrated in their lips and tongue to make sense of their world and the things in it. Your baby may spend a long time amusing herself by playing with her own hands and feet, even putting them in her mouth. This is all part of exploring and making sense of her world and helps integrate the senses of touch, taste and sight.

### Movement

Your baby is preparing to move. As her head control increases, she is able to push her head and shoulders up off the ground when on her tummy. She will then start to roll over – often preferring rolling in one direction at first and from front to back. You can encourage your baby to roll over by moving round to the side when she's watching you or making a noise over to one side of her. She will move her head, which changes her centre of gravity and helps her to roll. Once she has done it a few times accidentally, she will learn what she needs to do to roll over on purpose.

At some point during this stage your baby will be able to support her own head. This will vary depending on your baby, but she may possibly have some control over her head by two months and a strong control by six months. Once she has developed strong control, you can try bouncing her up and down with her gently standing on your lap – this is a great way to stimulate her leg muscle development. At first her legs may not provide much resistance but it won't take long for her to cushion the bounce by flexing her leg muscles and eventually learning to push off again as you lift her back up.

As her core muscles develop she may sit without support for a few seconds but will easily lose her balance. She won't mind toppling over as long as she doesn't hurt herself, so don't overreact and rush to help her unless she is in danger of hurting herself – make sure her landing is soft, as wriggling and rolling after toppling is hugely beneficial for her muscle development.

### Coordination

Babies' limbs tend to flail unpredictably for the first few weeks of life, but this soon refines as the beginnings of coordination become apparent. Your baby will reach for objects and start to intentionally bat at things. Her accuracy will improve rapidly as her sight and touch become integrated. You may notice that she starts to bring her hands together and is able to hold things in both hands, whereas before she would only use each hand individually.

### Teething

Just as things are starting to settle down, teething often comes along and bang goes your routine and sleep all over again.

## Thinking and communication

### Language

Initially babies won't use their vocal cords intentionally, other than in crying. However, as they become more aware of the world, they learn that they are capable of making sounds themselves. Your baby may initially be surprised at a sound she makes, but she will enjoy listening to her own voice and may gurgle contentedly for prolonged periods of time.

From around two months your baby will start to make noises, such as gurgles, squeals, coos and babbling sounds, in addition to crying, to express hunger, pleasure or pain. This is the start of intentional communication, and how you respond can have lasting effects on your baby.

Keep talking to her and make sure you pause, as in normal conversation, to encourage her to make noises in response. This promotes both attachment and communication skills. You can encourage your baby to make sounds by responding as if you have understood exactly what she is saying. When your baby trics to copy you, reflect the sounds back. Exaggerate the sounds and mouth movements and give positive reinforcement – e.g. smiling and repeating the action.

Try telling your baby what you are doing. For example, when you are changing her nappy, talk her through each step, maintaining eye contact when possible, and do the same when getting her dressed. Don't forget to incorporate some fun play activities (such as 'peekaboo' or gently blowing raspberries on her bare tummy, see pages 21, 23) to maximise everyone's enjoyment.

By around six months your baby will start to imitate your speech sounds, most likely starting with 'baba', 'dada'. It doesn't really matter what you attribute the babbling sounds to, but if you are consistent in what you think it means, the baby will learn to associate the different sounds with a reaction, and then communication begins in earnest.

Try recording your baby's gurgles and babbling noises for posterity – this phase doesn't last long.

Picture books and simple stories can be regularly read to your baby. Remember that at this age babies' attention spans are very short, but cuddling during story time will help them enjoy books and develop a life-long love of reading. Your baby will develop skills such as shared attention (i.e. she pays attention to what you are paying attention to) long before she understands a story, but the sound of your voice will help her develop language, and this may become an important part of her bedtime routine – as it is for many families.

### Thinking

Trial-and-error learning is just beginning as babies become aware that they have an effect on their environment and those around them. Your baby will try batting things to make them move, and enjoy interacting with others by copying a movement and expecting it to be mirrored back to her. Try opening and closing your mouth or sticking your tongue out and see if your baby copies you. If you see her doing something like that, reflect it back to her too, and try doing this together in front of a mirror. All of this stimulates your baby's cognitive development as she learns from everything she does and she will make sense of the world from both her successes and her frustrations.

## Social and emotional development

### *Attachment*
Your baby is able to recognise you by face and scent and she will also start to recognise her own name and turn towards you when you say it. All of this strengthens the bond between you and your baby. Avoid changing household products, especially laundry detergent and toiletries, as this will confuse your baby, and try not to wear too much perfume or deodorant as it is your natural smell that is most comforting to her.

Fear of unknown adults (also known as 'stranger anxiety') may begin around now; this is a natural part of the strengthening bond between you and your child. The best way to deal with clinginess at this age is to make sure your child feels very secure. Routines and consistency are important and will help your baby learn that you will come back even if you have to leave her for a while. Young babies have very short attention and memory spans and have not yet developed a concept called 'object permanence', so out of sight is very much out of mind. Therefore try not to keep popping in and out to check on a baby that was unhappy when you left, as you will just keep on upsetting her. Instead, to begin with, try to limit the number of times you leave and return to the baby within the same day if she really gets upset.

If you are away from your baby and worried about her settling, try leaving a soft piece of clothing you have just worn in the cot for her to cuddle up to. A T-shirt is ideal (make sure you don't leave anything like a scarf that could get wrapped around your baby and cause her harm).

### *Laughing*

Your baby is likely to start gurgling with pleasure at around 9 to 12 weeks, and may even show signs of giggles. At around 12 to 16 weeks giggling will be reactive as you make her laugh intentionally.

Her first proper chortle is a lovely moment and can make all the sleepless nights seem worthwhile. From this moment it is clear that your baby is able to experience and express utter joy. Laughter has a plethora of beneficial physiological effects – including releasing endorphins, reducing cortisol and so calming a baby, as well as boosting her immune system – so it needs to be celebrated and encouraged. Do not be afraid to make a fool of yourself if it elicits gorgeous giggles from your baby – in terms of attachment, nothing promotes bonding better than shared laughter.

## Playful Activities

Sensory play encourages a range of developmental skills including hand–eye coordination, motor control, curiosity, exploration and sensory integration (the connections formed between different parts of the brain when more than one sense is used in an activity). Play involving the senses also creates more connections between the different areas of the brain, which is believed to be beneficial for learning and memory in later life. All play and interaction with the world stimulates the senses in some way, but below are a few ideas that are particularly good for babies at this age as they engage more than one sense at a time.

Babies will still enjoy all of the play activities in the previous chapter and can have fun with these new ones, which will help stimulate all their senses.

### Floating scarves

To help your baby develop the ability to track movement with her eyes and integrate her senses of vision and touch, try scrunching up light pieces of material (e.g. chiffon). Throw the material up in the air and let it float gently down on to her. Don't remove the material immediately; let your baby experience the sensation of the material against her skin (making sure it is not covering her mouth or nose and won't stop her breathing).

## Bubbles

While your baby will not be able to blow bubbles herself, she will follow them with her eyes and experience the sensation of them landing and popping on her skin. Play with bubbles by waving your hands to create a draught and watch them change direction. Check they don't land in her eyes, blowing them out of the way if required.

## Make discovery rattles

Part-fill plastic bottles with dried beans, lentils or beads, ensure they are securely fastened and then shake. If different bottles make different sounds, show your baby which one you are picking up and shaking, so she learns to associate the sounds with the look of each rattle. Older siblings will enjoy doing this for the baby and can even decorate the bottles too.

## Massage

Massaging your baby promotes attachment and stimulates the touch receptors on her body, helping her become more aware of her limbs. Use items such as sponges, cotton wool and rubber gloves to touch her so she can feel other textures, but skin-to-skin touch is particularly powerful as it releases the powerful 'love hormone' oxytocin.

## Singing

Singing to your baby is really beneficial. She loves to hear familiar voices, and the rhythm and repetition will introduce her to the first stages of communication and language. Singing has a soothing effect on babies and so quiet lullabies before bed can help her relax and fall asleep.

Some parents feel awkward singing aloud and think because they can't sing in tune they shouldn't sing at all. Your child doesn't care what you sound like and no one else is listening, so take advantage of the opportunity to sing to someone who will enjoy it (the rewards it provides your child will be worth it).

### Reading

Although your baby is far from being old enough to understand books and their content, hearing you read can still be very beneficial.

Choose books that you can interact with and add noises and actions too. Those featuring animals and transport are good examples; you can 'moo' when there is a picture of a cow and 'brrrooom' with the car.

Some books have puppets or props attached or different textures for your baby to feel, which also aid interaction.

### Tummy time

Babies should be placed on their back to sleep in order to reduce the risk of sudden infant death syndrome (SIDS) or cot death; however, they need as much tummy time as possible in the day to strengthen their core stability and neck muscles. Tummy time can also reduce flat spots on the back of a baby's skull by relieving pressure on that part of the head. If a baby is on her back for long periods of time, the soft skull plates often move and create flat spots known as positional plagiocephaly or brachycephaly. If your baby does get this, don't panic: it usually corrects itself with time, but ensure she spends more time on her tummy during periods of play and do check with your GP if you are concerned.

There are plenty of play mats available that incorporate different textures and objects for play, but you can make your own if you are on a budget by putting different materials on a blanket for your baby to touch and explore – try fluffy cushions, shiny paper or even sandpaper. This is a great exercise as it stimulates your baby's curiosity and will encourage her to lift her head and shoulders to reach the objects, thus strengthening the core muscles needed for sitting, rolling, crawling and pulling herself up. As your baby approaches six months of age she should be able to lift her head, pushing up with her arms and balancing on her tummy.

## Bath-time fun

Bath time can be a parent's favourite time of the day (and not just because it is close to bedtime!) The safety aspect means you need to supervise your baby at all times. Play will occur naturally and is uninterrupted – this is real quality time for you and your baby. There is a wide range of bath toys available but there is nothing to stop you from improvising with empty yoghurt pots and squeezy bottles. The important thing is to get some toys in the bath that will aid play and learning while increasing the enjoyment of this special time for both parents and children. As your baby learns to sit up, bath time becomes even more fun and bath play opportunities are endless.

The range of bath-time toys available has increased dramatically in recent years and products such as stackable bath cups are great for helping your child build her confidence in water (using the cup as a shower or trying to fill it up by splashing), as well as enabling her to explore colour, size and volume, and improve her motor skills through stacking as she gets older. The simplicity of the cups enables them to be used in imaginative role play as cups or bowls, seats, hats, etc. This also means that they are suitable for a range of ages as children use them in different ways appropriate to their age and developmental stage.

Bath time is increasingly becoming a popular activity for dads. Many dads look forward to the end of their working day when they can get home and

play fun games with their baby in the bath. This works well as it also gives the mother some time away from the demands of a young child. Fathers tend to play more boisterously with their children than mothers do, and bath time provides a great opportunity for a bit of splashing and noisy play. Providing the child is supervised, she can be encouraged to splash around and put her face in the water to 'swim' or blow bubbles, all of which increases confidence and helps her learn to swim when the time comes.

A good bath time can aid a smooth bedtime routine as the children are already nice and warm and hopefully relaxed. This can make all the difference to behaviour the following day as a good night's sleep will make for a more reasonable and well-behaved child, with more energy and a healthy appetite. While lots of factors contribute to a child's development, the value of a fun, relaxing bath time should not be underestimated.

Safety is a major concern when children are in the bath, with regards to both the risk of drowning and the risk of scalding with hot water. There are many safety products available for bath time, including a fence which keeps children away from the tap end of the bath. However, instead of spending money buying all the safety equipment on the market, if you invest your time in playing with your child to help her enjoy bath time and understand the risks involved ('Don't touch the taps, they are hot'), the dangers diminish and the fun factor increases. It is also wise to turn the temperature on the boiler down to hand-hot – this saves money, benefits the environment and is the best way to make sure that if the baby touches the hot tap it will be unpleasantly hot but not dangerously so, thus minimising the risk of scalding.

A full-sized bath gives a very young baby the opportunity to kick and stretch out in a way that is not possible in a baby bath. There are a range of bath ramps or sponge mats which help keep your baby's head out of water while allowing her to kick and wave to her heart's content, allowing you a free hand to clean her. These are great and a lot smaller and easier to store than a baby bath. A folded-up towel makes a good substitute and helps solve travel problems when space is short.

The odd splash of water on your baby's face is good for improving water confidence and, as long as you are there to keep an eye on everything, you should not be afraid of letting your child enjoy the bath fully.

## Choosing Toys

Children at this age still don't really 'play' in the way they will in a few months' time. However, toys that are designed for this age group do stimulate senses and promote healthy development by encouraging interaction with others, which is important for attachment as well as social and emotional development.

Babies at this age are starting to be more aware of their environment and, although they are still largely unable to control the movement of their limbs, they will enjoy toys such as baby gyms, which have objects dangling down within reach of their flailing arms and legs. The movement or noise which results from the baby hitting or kicking (albeit unintentionally) will entertain her and aid development of skills such as concentration and an understanding of cause and effect.

As babies start grabbing things and putting them in their mouths, their motor development goes through a spurt. Anything that your baby can hold with her whole hand and which can be safely put in her mouth (lips and tongue are used to explore shape and texture more than hands in young babies) will encourage development (and will help soothe early teethers).

## Mirrors

Your baby is likely to be fascinated by what she can see in the mirror. She will gradually learn that she is the person she can see and will then take great delight in making movements and seeing them reflected back at her.

## Tummy-time toys

Textured play mats, and soft toys that won't hurt if rolled on to, provide stimulation during 'tummy time'. Noisy toys encourage your baby to move her head to the noise, and toys which are small enough to grasp will encourage her to reach out, lift her shoulders and move her arms.

## Teethers

Toys that have a teething element to them can provide relief for babies struggling with their painful gums. Even when babies are not in pain, multi-textured toys that can be explored with their lips and tongues will promote sensory stimulation and appeal to young babies.

Teethers that are cold provide more relief for sore gums so try keeping them in the fridge when not in use.

## Soft toys

Cuddly toys are beneficial for emotional development as babies respond to the softness and gain comfort from them. Soft toys also retain scents better than plastic or wooden toys and this provides familiarity and further comfort for your baby. More information on the value of soft toys can be found on pages 151–53. Try to buy more than one of your baby's favourite toys so it can be washed – this will also help avoid having a devastated child if one gets lost (but don't be surprised if your baby prefers the old smellier version!)

## Multi-sensory toys

These toys are designed to stimulate more than one sense at a time, such as textured rattles, musical light projectors and squeaky teether toys, are popular with parents of children in this age group. They help babies form connections that help with thought processes later in life.

## It Is Not Always Easy – Troubleshooting Tips

### 'My baby doesn't like being on her tummy'

It can be difficult to encourage tummy time when your baby seems reluctant and starts getting upset. However, tummy time is key for muscle development and prepares a baby for crawling, so it is important to ensure your baby does spend some time on her front. There are a number of things to try that can help your baby:

- Once she is able to support her own head, prop her up using a thin cushion or rolled up towel under her chest so she is not flat. This will free up her arms and make it easier for her to move them around, grabbing things and exploring her environment.
- Lie flat on your back and place your baby on your chest so she sees your face when she lifts her head. You can lie at an angle (e.g. on pillows), which will make it easier for your baby to push herself up.
- Lie your baby on her front, with her head on an unbreakable mirror – the coolness of the mirror will encourage her to lift her head up, and the reflection will grab her attention and prolong the time that she holds her head up.

### 'I think my baby may have problems with her vision'

Your baby should be able to see you and close-up objects from birth. She should also be able to distinguish different colours (particularly bolder and bright colours). If your baby is showing any signs of regular squinting or crossed eyes, isn't showing any signs of following a moving object in front of her, or is uninterested in looking at bright or contrasting coloured objects, seek advice from your health visitor or GP.

To check for any sight problems in a playful way, place a brightly coloured toy in front of your baby and slowly move it from side to side. See if her eyes follow the toy.

## 10 Fun Things to Do with Your Child

1. Take her swimming.
2. Tickle her face with a feather.
3. Go for a walk outside somewhere new.
4. Attend a local music or story-time class.
5. Read her a story.
6. Attend a baby group.
7. Let her look at herself in the mirror.
8. Blow bubbles to her and let her watch them.
9. Dance around the kitchen with her in your arms.
10. Play in the grass.

## Making Memories

What multi-sensory activities does your baby most enjoy?

.......................................................................................................

.......................................................................................................

.......................................................................................................

What is your favourite song to sing to your baby?

.......................................................................................................

What would you like to remember most about this phase?

.......................................................................................................

.......................................................................................................

.......................................................................................................

What advice do you wish you had taken?

.......................................................................................................

.......................................................................................................

What advice are you glad you ignored?

.......................................................................................................

.......................................................................................................

Does your baby seem to prefer toys that are visually stimulating, or those that make sounds?

.......................................................................................................

.......................................................................................................

What is your baby's favourite toy?

.......................................................................................................

## Your Notes

.......................................................................................................

.......................................................................................................

.......................................................................................................

.......................................................................................................

.......................................................................................................

.......................................................................................................

.......................................................................................................

.......................................................................................................

**play**

..........................................................................................

..........................................................................................

..........................................................................................

..........................................................................................

..........................................................................................

..........................................................................................

..........................................................................................

..........................................................................................

..........................................................................................

..........................................................................................

# Chapter Three
# Fun with Food
# (6–12 Months)

As babies pass the six-month mark most will be weaning and the issue of food is at the forefront of their parents' minds. Meals and nutrition are very much at the heart of many family units, providing wonderful opportunities for bonding, communication and passing on family values. Making mealtimes fun will promote healthy attitudes towards food and nutrition, as well as stimulating development across all of the senses.

As childhood obesity is still on the rise (in the US children born in the last 10 years have a shorter life expectancy than their parents due to the likelihood of them developing diabetes and heart disease[2]), promoting healthy attitudes to food and nutrition from the start – an area that causes many difficulties – is vital.

As well as looking at the development of eating in babies – from weaning to consuming the same foods as the rest of the family – this chapter puts children's engagement with food in the wider context of the development that occurs during these months.

**play**

## Food and Drink

Weaning is a gradual process and the key to success is to go at your baby's own pace. She will still be getting most of the nutrition she needs from her usual breast milk or formula. Try a range of foods, starting with vegetables, to avoid developing an overly sweet tooth early on. Remember not to leave your baby or toddler eating unsupervised as choking can be common in young children – babies have very narrow windpipes.

Having fun with food will not just help your child develop an interest in eating but will also allow her to use and understand her senses further. Allowing her to explore her food through touch as well as taste can introduce her to textures, temperatures and an abundance of smells. Weaning can be messy, so prepare the area well, protecting furniture, floors and clothing. Let your baby have fun and enjoy her mealtimes – manners will come later.

Your baby will be starting to take water from a cup at this stage. Cups with lids will help prevent spillages, and as children get a little older offering a plastic cup without a lid (ideally only with a small amount of water in to start with) will encourage your baby to develop more control over her arm muscles and improve her hand–eye coordination.

As your baby gets older the texture of her food will become lumpier and you can introduce finger foods. Some parents adopt an approach called baby-led weaning, where babies are offered finger food from the start. This can be successful if you continue to breastfeed or give your baby formula milk past the age of six months, but for babies who are difficult to satisfy with milk only, baby food provides digestible nutrition that stimulates taste buds and encourages exploration of taste and texture of food. Most parents take a mixed approach, offering finger food and purees to children from six months.

Try to keep your child's diet as varied as possible – the more variety she eats as a baby, the less fussy she will be later in life. Introducing the type of foods you eat as a family early on will make mealtimes less stressful in the future and promote family meals, which are hugely beneficial to a child's social and emotional development throughout her childhood. Be sensitive to the possibility of your child having heightened sensory perception. Strong tastes may not appeal to young children and spicy foods can cause discomfort, both on the way in and out!

## Making mealtimes playful

Mealtimes are not just about nutrition. They are a great learning time for your baby as she is still trying to understand her new world. Your child will learn so much through practical involvement and play, and mealtimes are no different. Promoting a healthy attitude towards foods can be started from this age so it is important for mealtimes to be fun and engaging.

There are many textures, smells, colours and noises that are absorbed by your child through sight, taste, touch, smell and sound. Although it can be messy and you may not want to encourage playing with food at every meal, allow your child a little freedom with her hands to explore. Let her squish mashed sweet potato, feeling the warm, soft texture and seeing it ooze through her fingers. Offering your child natural yoghurt or cooled stewed apple will give her the comparison of different temperatures. As she gets older, and more solids are introduced, further textures can be explored. For example, pasta, rice, peas and chunks of pineapple are all different colours, shapes and textures, and will make mealtimes far more varied and enjoyable.

Choosing foods with distinctive aromas, such as cheese, strawberries, fish or casseroles, will help your child recognise foods using her sense of smell. Colour can also be a huge draw to a child of this age, so be creative and make her dinner look interesting. Carrots, tomatoes or peas can make her dinner bright and colourful. As finger foods are introduced you will be able to get even more creative.

## What to Look Out for During this Stage

### Physical and sensory development

#### *Movement*
Movement is now getting easier as your baby's muscles are developing rapidly. She is gaining in strength and will want to put her new skills to the test and gain more freedom.

Sitting without support is more easily achieved as she progresses towards crawling and walking. She may start to lunge forward in order to grab something or start crawling to get objects which are close by.

Standing while holding on to something is a new and exciting skill that your baby may try to do at every opportunity, and she will love being on her feet. She will be pulling herself up on everything she can reach and it may now be time to 'baby proof' your home and put anything you don't want her to get hold of out of sight and certainly out of reach.

As your child gains confidence in standing she will start to cruise around furniture, using it as support. She will still be quite wobbly so will need support but you can encourage further movement by holding her hands and walking her around or putting things she wants to play with just out of reach to encourage self-movement. Baby walkers/push-along toys are also useful at assisting walking and will help rest your hands and back.

While most babies start to walk between 12 and 18 months, some walk as early as 9 months and some not until after 18 months. Once your child has accomplished a few steps there will no stopping her and she will want to explore everywhere. Try to resist the urge to get competitive with other parents regarding the age your child walks as she will do it at her own pace and will be developing other skills in the meantime.

### Coordination

In a sitting position your child can reach for objects she finds interesting, grip them and drag them towards her, more often than not putting them in her mouth to explore them (this can also be a sign of teething). Other signs of her developing coordination include pointing at objects and banging things together.

She will also progress from whole-hand grabbing to picking things up with her thumb and forefinger – the 'pincer grasp'. This fine motor control is the skill your child will need to hold a pen or pencil and be able to write, so it is important to facilitate its development.

### Touch and taste
Your baby will love to put everything in her mouth at this stage so it is important to remove anything that is not suitable or that might be a choking hazard.

### Teething
Some babies may have already started teething but the most common age for them to cut their first tooth is around now (although it is not uncommon for children to have their first tooth close to 24 months).

Although some babies seem to teethe without suffering from sore gums, the majority will find it very painful and your baby will likely be crying, seem irritable and possibly have high temperatures during teething. If your child suffers from these symptoms you can use any of the products available to help soothe the pain. Teething toys (especially the ones that can be made cold in the fridge) can be good at easing the pain, as can teething gels, rusks and age-appropriate paracetamol to reduce temperatures.

## Thinking and communication

### Thinking
Trial-and-error learning is the most basic form of logic. Babies are starting to experiment around this age and are absorbing information all the time. Your child will be trying to make different

noises and actions, often imitating those around her, and will know how to get her caregiver's attention.

Her own attention will be fleeting and she will enjoy the surprise of novelty as her short-term memory has not yet developed. Out of sight is very much out of mind, which explains why peekaboo (see page 21) is such a popular game with children of this age.

Your child's understanding of her world will be developing as she is getting more freedom through her newly found movement, and is therefore gaining more stimulation and access to new experiences. She will be absorbing information at a rapid pace and using her findings to think and learn.

### Language

Communication takes many forms at this age and it can be a particularly exciting time for you all as your baby starts to talk. Words are often unidentifiable to start with but you will soon get to know your own baby's language and understand that, for example, when she says 'ings' she actually means 'swings'. Try to write these new words down as they are often funny to refer back to when she is older.

It is also important not to forget the other forms of communication that she will be developing. Non-verbal communication will still be her main channel so don't ignore the gestures and signals that she gives out, even when she doesn't know she is doing them. It will take a long time before her language is able to accurately describe what she wants or explain how she feels, but as parents we are programmed to read the non-verbal cues, so trust your instinct to interpret what she is telling you.

Your baby will use gestures to help others understand what she wants and needs, pointing to objects of interest and maybe making noises to grab your attention. To encourage speech development, when you see her pointing and wanting something, repeat the word back to her. For example, if she points to her water bottle, as you pass it to her say, 'Here is your drink.' This will encourage her to say 'Drink' the next time she wants it.

Gestures that she can manage will also include waving 'Hello' and 'Goodbye' and putting her finger to her lips to indicate quiet. These all come from imitating you, so the more of them you do, the more your child will copy.

You may want to take the use of gestures even further by doing 'baby signing'. This method of communication uses simple hand gestures to allow your baby to let you know what she is wanting before she is able to express herself verbally. She can learn signs to express hunger, a need for milk and a dirty nappy, plus many more. While baby signing is great for children with language difficulties and can reduce tantrums and frustrations, make sure it isn't overused in case it delays her speech. Saying the word as you sign it is a good way to make sure that language development isn't compromised.

Your baby will start to recognise and respond to her own name. 'Dada' and 'Mama' may be regularly said now, but not necessarily in the correct context. At first your baby may say it to both of her parents indiscriminately, then eventually she will understand who 'dada' is and who 'mama' is and say the correct name to the correct parent.

## Social and emotional development

Your child will now be able to imitate others' actions. This is the beginning of social interaction and, as well as aiding the development of positive traits such as empathy, it will form the basis of friendships later in life. Games such as peekaboo are particularly good for this age group as they can learn to copy the actions and so play the game too (until this age, babies are largely observers of adults playing these types of games).

### Attachment

Your child will recognise her primary carers and will generally be at her happiest and most confident when she is with them. However, she will also be aware of her secondary carers with whom she has regular contact and feels safe and secure around (i.e. her grandparents or a childminder).

Between 6 and 12 months your baby may start to show anxieties towards people she doesn't recognise or become upset when left in an environment she is not familiar with. This is a sign of secure attachment and, while it can be frustrating and even traumatic for parents, it is an important phase in your child's emotional development. Try introducing a cuddly toy if she doesn't already have one. These can be useful when you are not around as she will develop an attachment to a particular soft toy and it can be taken wherever she goes; this will help to comfort her when she is distressed.

## Playful Activities

Your baby will continue to enjoy games mentioned in previous chapters and, as she is more able, can get more involved with new activities.

## Food art

Turn your baby's plate into a picture – such as a rainbow or a face – using brightly coloured foods. She will love to see what you will be creating next. Cucumber, raw peppers, raisins, grapes and tomatoes are all great for creating designs or shapes. (Please note that small round foods such as tomatoes and grapes should be cut in half to avoid risk of choking and you should never leave your child unattended while eating.)

## Singing the next step

There are songs about food, such as 'Oranges and Lemons' (see page 198), which she will enjoy hearing. 'Head, Shoulders, Knees and Toes' (see page 198) is good to sing during mealtimes, as when you get to the 'mouth' part you can stop and she can eat a mouthful before carrying on the song. The same goes for 'Little Miss Muffet' (see page 199).

Non-food-related songs that have great actions and noises can include 'The Wheels on the Bus' or 'Old MacDonald Had a Farm' (see pages 199 and 200).

## Kitchen orchestra

Your baby will watch you preparing her food and will enjoy using some of the utensils or pans to make herself a kitchen orchestra. For example, a spoon and plastic tub make a lovely drum.

## Chase

Try coming down to crawling level on the floor and playing chase around the house. Your baby will love both being chased and also trying to chase you. This simple game will not only help to develop her gross motor skills but it will strengthen muscles, encourage movement and she will start really giggling too (the benefits of which are endless – see page 39).

## Clapping

Up until now her clapping movements may have been two fists hitting together or one fist hitting against an open hand; however, as her coordination is improves, she will start being able to clap her hands together properly. Games and rhymes that involve clapping will help her strengthen her arm muscles and she will enjoy hearing the sound she can make with her hands.

## Copy me

Your baby will love to watch you make new facial expressions or movements and eventually will start trying to copy you. Facing her, start by poking your tongue out, encouraging her to do the same (this may take a while, but she will eventually get it). Once she is sticking her tongue out, smile at her and encourage her to smile back. As she gets more advanced you can try anything: pointing to body parts, rolling a ball to her, putting a plastic cup over your hand, etc.

## Tumble tower

Stack plastic cups on top of each other to build a tall tower (this can be done with wooden bricks too) and get her to push them over. She will love watching them tumble down into a pile. Keep doing this (although be careful, she may have you there for hours) and she will love it, giggling more and more as she gets used to them falling over. This develops hand-eye co-ordinaton.

## Treasure touch box

Create your own texture treasury with items that are safe for her to play with, such as wooden spoons, ribbons, an unbreakable mirror, straws, a large sponge, plastic bottles or anything else you can find around the house. Use these as props for stories or to help your baby explore. If you are making your own treasure basket using household items, make sure its use is properly supervised and you don't leave her alone with items that could cause her harm.

## Hand and foot printing

This activity is messy but can be great fun for both your baby and yourself! Make sure you protect your floor or table with newspaper or plastic sheeting, then get a large plastic plate and fill it with lots of paint. Allow your baby to explore the paint with her hands (watching she doesn't put it in her mouth) – the texture of thick, gloopy paint will be fascinating. Once she is well covered in paint, use her hands or feet to take prints on paper or canvas. These can be great mementos for you and your family and can even be used to make 'thank you' cards for gifts received on her first birthday.

## Choosing Toys

Toys such as stacking cups or bricks, musical instruments, picture books, wheeled toys, activity centres, bath toys, shape sorters and puppets are all appropriate for this age group.

Toys that can be fixed to a buggy, high chair or baby gym will prevent the frustration that babies feel when they drop a toy and cannot reach it. When sitting on the floor, they can see the toys they drop and will make attempts to retrieve them, which makes it less demanding on parents and more likely that children will be able to entertain themselves for longer periods of time, although concentration spans in children of this age are still very short.

### Teethers

Most babies will be teething during this period and textured toys which can act as teethers are very popular. The ones that are suitable for refrigerating can be particularly good for pain relief.

### Play gyms

If babies are not sitting up yet at this age, toys that encourage muscle development in the back are beneficial. Baby gyms that can be converted into sitting play gyms come into their own around now. Door bouncers and play activity centres can also aid sitting as they strengthen core stability as well as strengthening leg muscles.

### Push-along and moving toys

As children become mobile, toys with wheels that they can push (such as a brick trolley) will provide them with an opportunity to practise walking.

Small toys with wheels, balls and other toys which have a tendency to move away from your child are also beneficial in aiding development of movement, as your child will be motivated to follow them once they are out of reach.

## Home-made activity stations

As a baby moves around her environment she is able to experience the world in her own way and will access a range of experiences that were not available before. Sometimes it's difficult for parents to adjust to having a baby on the move and activity stations can be useful for keeping a baby in one place for a short while. Choose a low table she can easily reach and place everyday objects suitable for her to play with such as baby-safe plastic cutlery, a plastic bowl, an old telephone, a small saucepan and a packet of baby wipes. To avoid boredom and maintain her engagement, change the objects on top regularly and don't leave them there for too long. As with all objects that are not made as toys, you need to supervise their use and make sure they are safe and suitable for your child to play with.

## Boxes

Babies of this age like to put things in and out of containers, so a tub of bricks in a plastic box is likely to be very appealing, and the repetitive action is great for the development of neural pathways. You can change the contents of the box regularly to keep your baby interested.

## Snuggle toy

Using a soft toy, hold it high and bring it down quickly to give her lots of kisses and tickle her neck. This helps her to focus and follow objects and will encourage her to laugh aloud.

## It Is Not Always Easy – Troubleshooting Tips

### 'My child isn't crawling'

Not all children will crawl: some 'bum shuffle' along the floor, some 'commando crawl' across the floor on their tummies, while others simply go straight from sitting to standing and then walking.

There are a few simple steps you can do with your child to encourage crawling. Place your baby on her front regularly (see 'tummy time' on page 42); she will start to lift her head off the floor and show interest in objects ahead of her. If you think she is ready and strong enough to crawl, try helping her to support her weight on her arms. Placing a toy out of reach but very visible may encourage her to crawl to get it. This may take several practices.

When socialising with other children who crawl, ensure your child can see their movements. She may be curious enough to imitate them.

If you have any serious concerns over your child's physical development, it is important to seek medical advice from your doctor or health visitor as early as possible.

## 10 Fun Things to Do with Your Child

1. Have a buggy race in the park.
2. Take a trip on a railway.
3. Swing her on a swing.
4. Help her dance to music.
5. Make noises with musical instruments.
6. Play in a paddling pool.
7. Play in a ball pool.
8. Let her empty a box of tissues or baby wipes.

9. Take her on a bouncy castle.
10. Take a trip on a bus.

## Making Memories

When did your baby's first tooth appear?

.......................................................................................................

What is your favourite playful activity?

.......................................................................................................

What is your favourite meal to make for your baby?

.......................................................................................................

What is your baby's favourite finger food?

.......................................................................................................

What foods does your baby seem to dislike?

.......................................................................................................

.......................................................................................................

What is your baby's favourite household object to play with?

.......................................................................................................

## Your Notes

..................................................................................................

..................................................................................................

..................................................................................................

..................................................................................................

..................................................................................................

..................................................................................................

..................................................................................................

..................................................................................................

..................................................................................................

..................................................................................................

..................................................................................................

..................................................................................................

..................................................................................................

..................................................................................................

..................................................................................................

..................................................................................................

..................................................................................................

# Chapter Four
# On the Move
# (12–18 Months)

As babies move into their second year they continue to develop rapidly. Big changes such as first words and first steps can make this a very rewarding time for parents.

But this age can also be challenging. Your child is mobile enough to get herself into potentially dangerous situations but does not yet have the knowledge or language skills to understand what she is doing. This is where evolution really could have helped parents out with an extra pair of hands and eyes in the back of their heads!

Encouraging movement during this time opens up all sorts of opportunities for development that your child doesn't get when sedentary. Your child will be gaining valuable experiences, increasing her engagement with people and exploring her world on a completely different level, while developing muscle strength, coordination and stamina.

As children grow physically stronger their sense of adventure and desire to explore are stimulated. Your child will become interested in everything and everyone, and it can feel like she is continuously on the go.

This is the perfect time to embed healthy amounts of activity into your child's daily routine, which will promote life-long health and well-being. Obviously, it is much healthier for a child to be active all day, go to bed early, sleep well and then wake up the following day raring to go, rather than flopping on the sofa after an activity and staying there for hours and then waking several times in the night. This is the stage when the power of play can really start to be seen and appreciated, and when parents can benefit both themselves and their children by balancing their children's play diets.

## What to Look Out for During this Stage

### Physical and sensory development

*Senses*

Children's senses are continually stimulated in this busy, vibrant world, and now your child is moving she will be stimulating her senses even more with novel experiences.

Sights and smells on walks around the garden and touching objects around the house all encourage her movement and continue to develop her sensory integration. Your toddler's world will be opening up much more to all sorts of new opportunities, and she will be using all five senses to help her understand and explore her world further. This type of exploration will lead to further vital developments in the form of language, creativity, imagination and cognitive development.

Allowing your child to learn through playing and doing is really valuable. She is much more likely to remember information she has learnt practically through her senses, rather than being told facts.

She will have used sight, touch and possibly language to do things for herself. This multi-modal experience will result in learning being much more memorable.

Try to incorporate as many activities that use your child's five senses as often as possible. Provide opportunities for her to make use of her newfound mobility – e.g. walking to the shops instead of using the car or, if you are in a rush, taking a tricycle to speed her up. Point out the different smells around the house and garden, and let her play outside and feel the plants, leaves and soil.

### *Movement*

Discovering the joy of climbing is exciting for your child, although it can be nerve-racking for you. Be extra vigilant by not leaving her alone with anything she can climb on and fall off – for example, sofas or coffee tables. Stairs are particularly fascinating at the moment and she will try to clamber up them at any given opportunity. Stair gates can give parents comfort, but the earlier children learn to use stairs safely the better, so encourage your child to climb the stairs herself with you behind her or holding her hand.

As with learning any new skill, there will be mistakes and your child will naturally fall and hurt herself, but this is all part of learning. Do not overreact to a fall but help her up and carry on as normal. Many toddlers cry because the noise made by those supervising the play startles them rather than because they have particularly hurt themselves. Make sure the environment is safe (e.g. no sharp objects or big steps) and then let your toddler have fun as she learns to move around.

Finding large, safe, open spaces where toddlers can run about and explore the outdoor environment is great. Encouraging your child to move to get balls, push a walker, etc., will strengthen her muscles – particularly those in the legs and feet – and improve her coordination and balance.

Your child will also become more aware of sound and music around her and she will inevitably start to move and dance in time to the beat, especially if she sees you or older siblings doing this. This is wonderful for promoting rhythm, strength and creativity and, as with all of these skills, the earlier your child experiences them the more easily she will develop them.

### Motor control

Your child will now be able to make a mark on paper using a chunky pencil, crayon or paintbrush. Her whole hand grasp will be more secure and the muscles will be strengthening rapidly. Now is the time for imagination and creativity to be encouraged through art and drawing! Her pincer grip (between her thumb and forefinger) will be getting stronger and it is an important skill to encourage, as it is required for many everyday tasks, such as holding a pen, using cutlery for eating and fastening zips and buttons.

### Food and drink

Finger foods can be more widely introduced now, as your child will enjoy feeding herself. As most things in her hands enter her mouth anyway, this is usually the same with food and she should find this no problem at all. Do remember that finger foods are potentially choking hazards so never leave your child unattended when eating and prepare all foods according to her capabilities.

Given her newfound mobility, now is a good time to make rules about sitting down to eat and not letting your child walk around with food. This will save you a lot of time clearing up (no one wants to find mouldy raisins under the sofa!) as well as reducing the risk of choking.

Using a spoon or fork and having a good amount of control over the utensil is now possible, although fingers are sometimes still preferable, especially with messy and different textures in new foods that look so much fun to play with. Offering your child raisins and other small pieces of food will encourage the pincer grip.

If she hasn't done so already you may notice that your child starts to develop fussiness towards certain foods, suddenly taking a dislike to something she has previously enjoyed. It is frustrating when you have spent ages in the kitchen, but try not to take it personally and don't assume it is a permanent dislike. Keep offering her a variety of other tastes and textures on a regular basis.

With all the focus on childhood obesity and eating disorders, parents can feel anxious about their child's diet but this may end up contributing to fussiness. It is not uncommon for a child to use food as a vehicle for exerting some control over their world. Children who are healthy will eat if they are hungry, and by this age there are no serious consequences of not eating much at one meal. Resist the urge to offer different food choices, it is not going to harm your child if she has to wait until the next mealtime before eating something as long as she gets plenty of water to drink. If this is the last meal of the day, you may want to offer a glass of milk or a small snack just before bedtime to avoid night-time waking from hunger.

There are fewer incidences of fussy eating in families who have their meals together in a relaxed manner, all eating the same food, so do this when you can and avoid letting children eat in front of a screen. There is a big difference between an occasional treat picnic in front of a film, and children habitually eating their meals in front of the television. Eating together promotes attachment, communication and provides an opportunity for parents to pass on family values and traditions to their children. Making family mealtimes the norm will reap huge rewards.

## Thinking and communication

### Language

Your child's language skills will be rapidly increasing. She will start to use some words appropriately but will have a limited repertoire that she will use to convey all of her desires, opinions and requests. 'No' may become your child's favourite word. Saying 'no' to your almost every request is not uncommon, but at this age it doesn't necessarily mean no. Children don't have a wide range of vocabulary so your child may use 'no' to cover everything from 'no', 'absolutely not', to 'wait, I don't understand', 'maybe' or 'not yet'. Don't overreact to 'no' – if you pay lots of attention to it, the chances are she will say it all the more. There will be other words that your child will use to cover a wider range of communication messages than adults, so remember that what your child says and what she means may differ to what you would mean when using the same words. This refines as she develops.

Your child may start to say 'Hello' and 'Goodbye' of her own accord when greeting or leaving and will add gestures such as waving or blowing a kiss.

It is a good idea to promote politeness; saying 'thank you' or 'Ta' when she is given anything lays the foundations for future manners.

Non-verbal communication is still very important at this age so don't forget to pay attention to her actions as much as her words.

Your child will also be becoming more aware of how to express her wants and needs effectively, combining her own known words and sounds with gestures to help you understand. For example, she may point to a cup and say, 'Milk.' You can promote her language development by adding a few more words to make a whole sentence and repeat this back to her as a question and answer, such as, 'Please can I have some milk?', 'Yes, of course you can.'

Having a select few favourite words that children use regularly is common and this will expand as she becomes more confident with speech. You may want to record or make a note of these favourite words or phrases as it is amazing how quickly you will forget them once her language abilities are more mature.

Communicate with your child as frequently as possible. Reading lots of books to her and talking to her as you go about your daily business will all help your child learn to talk. Use a variety of words to really encourage her language to grow – the few single words she knows will quickly become many and will soon be combined to form sentences.

### Listening

The other key element of communication, and one that is often overlooked, is listening. Ensure you actively listen to your child, even if there is not much sense in what she is saying, and she will learn to listen too. Active listening involves eye contact and appropriate responses to your child's communication, including questions and gestures that show her that you're really listening.

As the NSPCC points out, some children can't always put their feelings into words, so to truly listen to them you need to pay attention to their actions and behaviour too. Listening to children has a big impact; those who are listened to are usually well adjusted and self-confident, but those whose needs are ignored can become withdrawn or difficult and can suffer from low self-esteem.[3]

As your child's listening skills develop, she will be able to respond to a direction like 'Sit down'. Listening to stories will help develop her comprehension and listening skills further.

### Thinking

Your child's thinking skills will be leaping ahead at this stage. Following a two-step command will be achievable – for example, 'Can you pick the ball up and put it in the toy box?'

Her interest in just about everything she can see is really growing now and she will be exploring everywhere. Cupboards and drawers can be particularly interesting and it may be worthwhile investing in child safety locks for any cupboards that aren't suitable for tiny hands to empty.

Animals are fascinating to your child and she will love to look at them in books, possibly being able to point to the particular animals when asked. She will be starting to recognise everyday ones such as cats and dogs, trying to 'woof' like a dog or 'meow' like a cat, which helps develop intonation and expression within language.

Your child's attention span is still very limited. Although she may seem fascinated by something one minute, she will be looking for a new source of entertainment the next. Simple jigsaw puzzles can be really useful at this age for developing her concentration skills, as can imaginative role play. Walking around a wood pretending to look for fairies and elves under the mushrooms will really keep her focus and help to strengthen not only her imagination and creativity but also her attention span.

Children of this age will be using everyday objects correctly and start recognising 'cause and effect' – for example, banging a drum with her fist makes a loud noise and tipping her bowl upside down makes a mess.

## Social and emotional development

### Laughter

Laughter has, for a long time, been linked to many health benefits, as discussed on page 39. Although your child will have been laughing for a few months, at this age she will be able to really giggle and enjoy funny situations. YouTube has lots of videos of babies giggling uncontrollably and the amount of hits these videos receive is testament to how much we enjoy seeing and hearing babies laugh.

Of course, these benefits are not limited to your child, as a baby's laughter can be catching and you too can end up in fits of giggles just hearing her, so the health benefits will have a positive effect on you too! There are plenty of games you can play with your child to encourage laughter; she will love you chasing her around pretending to be the tickle monster or gently throwing her up into the air and catching her. As she gets older she will understand how she can make other people laugh too. This boosts confidence and promotes her social interactions.

### Attachment

Imitating you and others is a key learning tool this age group will be using. Your child will increase her understanding of the world by watching everyone around her and she will start to copy everything she sees. While this phase can be challenging for parents, it is an important stage of developing attachment. Parents often report that their child wants the 'grown-up' version of household objects, especially keys and phones, and cannot be palmed off with toy replicas. This can be frustrating for parents who are permanently searching for these items. One compromise may be to get an old bunch of real keys and pretend to use it for a while. Your child will hopefully accept these as substitutes for your own items. However, all toys are safety-tested to very high standards (only food and medicines are subject to more rigorous safety standards), whereas old keys and phones are not designed for children.

### Tantrums

Temper tantrums can occur more frequently as your baby becomes an older toddler and gets frustrated due to an imbalance between her thought and language skills. Your child's brain is telling her what she wants or needs yet she doesn't have the capabilities to express this to an adult correctly or can't comprehend why she is not allowed it. Staying calm, trying to distract her with another activity while communicating with her can all help to avoid conflict and tantrums. However, if there is no way of settling the situation, it may be beneficial to let her have the tantrum without interfering (ensuring she is safe at all times), allowing her to eventually calm herself down. This can be emotionally difficult for you as a parent but be assured there will be no lasting negative impact on your child from seeing out a temper tantrum.

### Development of identity

Your child will enjoy gazing at her reflection in a mirror or even the glass of a shop window as she will recognise herself by now, and may be engrossed for long periods by her reflection.

Mirrors can be fascinating for your child and really help to develop her concentration span. Ask her to point to her different features in the mirror and help her to understand her individual identity and yours.

## Travelling with young children

Travelling with babies and toddlers requires careful planning and flexibility on your part and you should be realistic about the needs of your child. Allow enough time for a leisurely journey with frequent stops to give your child a chance to exercise and work off excess energy.

Travelling can help children become more open to new and different people, places and ideas. Their natural curiosity also makes travel a great educational experience and seeing the world through the eyes of your child is a rich experience for you too. The journey can be stressful for parents but by seeing it as a key part of the trip, and allowing regular breaks, it can become much more enjoyable for all.

You can try to avoid problems by having a range of activities up your sleeve and planning the timing of your journey around sleep and mealtimes. Try the following tips to make your journeys more fun filled, so the hours of 'Are we nearly there yet' are left behind.

- Invest in some colouring or sticker books, which your child can scribble on.

- Wheelie suitcases that she can ride on will make manoeuvring around an airport more fun, and you can store her books and crayons inside.

- Traditional games never wear out and 'I spy' and 'First person to see …' still offer hours of fun for the car (see page 85 for these games). Take advantage of the scenery outside, pointing out animals in the fields. For example, 'first person to see a cow …'

- It is difficult to travel light with children, but imaginative packing pays off. Consider a separate suitcase for your child. Making a checklist as you pack and taping the list to the inside of the suitcase might prevent her favourite teddy bear from being left behind in a hotel room.

- Dress your child in old, comfortable clothes for travelling. If you want her to look fresh and neat when you arrive at your destination, pack extra clothes for changing into at the last minute, or have her wear a large bib or sleeveless apron during the journey.

- Just remember that a lovely holiday in an exotic location may sound idyllic but the effects of the break may be short-lived if the return journey with a restless toddler is too long. Make sure you plan time to recover from the journey before getting back into everyday life.

## Playful Activities

Your child will have favourite games and toys by now, but she is always ready to discover new ones. Here are some fun activities that she may start to enjoy in addition to those from previous chapters.

### Shape sorters

Your child will love organising shapes into the correct holes. You may need to assist her to start with, although it won't take her long to master this. This is a great activity for strengthening her fine motor and problem-solving skills.

### Bouncy, bouncy

Bounce her gently up and down on your knees. If she wants more, then bounce her a couple of times on your knee and on the third time open your legs and gently let her drop slightly through. You can also pair these actions up with a song such as 'Humpty Dumpty' (see page 201) or 'This is how the … rides' (see page 201).

### Retrieve the toy

Leave her favourite toy out of reach and encourage her to walk and get it. Later, leave the toy on the floor to encourage bending over, picking it up and then standing up again without losing balance. This is all achievable at this age and is hugely beneficial to her emerging skills of balance and coordination.

### Feeding a doll

This can be particularly useful at mealtimes, especially if your child is a fussy eater. She can feed dolly while you feed her. Provide her with plastic props to aid this action, such as a spoon, bowl and tissue to wipe her dolly's mouth when she spills it.

## Dancing

Dance around the house to music with your child in your arms – she will love the bouncing and twirling movement. Provide a variety of music such as pop, classical and her favourite nursery rhymes.

## Mud pies

This is a fantastically cheap and easy activity that offers hours of fun and promotes creativity. Mud is messy but always a hit and encourages children to play outside even when the weather isn't great. All she requires is a bowl, water and an area of mud.

Find a patch of mud in your garden that you are happy for your child to dig in. Make the mud wet so that it becomes a little sticky. Fill a bowl with the mud and pat it down hard. Tip the bowl upside down to create a 'mud pie'. You can use a beach bucket if you want to make 'mud castles'. Children will need supervision on this activity to ensure they don't put the mud into their mouths.

## Ball games

Roll or throw a ball to her, encouraging her to do the same back to you. Get her to chase after it if it rolls away from her. As her movement gets stronger and her confidence grows she can start kicking balls around the garden or park, but don't expect her to be able to do this yet.

## Hide and seek

Your child will love to hunt out hidden objects. Play hide and seek with her around the house – you can also hide 'teddy' in places and ask her to hunt him out. Make sure you don't make it too hard for her to find or she will quickly lose interest, and at this age do it together and lead her until she gets the idea.

## 'I spy' (toddler version)

This is a great game for car journeys and travelling. The first person says 'I spy something that…' ('has eyes' or 'is green', for example). The toddler then has to point to something that fits the description.

## 'First person to see …'

Another great one for journeys, this involves everyone looking for a named object. One player says 'First person to see…' then chooses something, such as a red car. The other players have to look for this and shout out when they see it. The winner then gets to choose the next object. Good items to look out for include different animals grazing in fields, numbers (featured on signs), different coloured lorries or cars, aeroplanes and bicycles.

## Choosing Toys

### Building blocks

Your baby is likely to be able to start stacking blocks on top of each other, even if it is only a couple to start with. Building towers and knocking them over again and again is likely to be fun for children at this age and is developmentally fabulous. It opens up opportunities to learn colours and counting, and each time the blocks get stacked, your child's motor control will be that little bit more sophisticated.

## High-chair toys

Toys that clip or stick on to your child's high chair can be great at distracting and keeping your child's attention at mealtimes, encouraging her to stay happily at the family meal table.

## Ride-ons

Toys that your child sits on with her feet just touching the floor, enabling her to push herself along, are great at this age as they will strengthen her leg muscles and core stability, as well as improving balance, concentration and coordination.

## Musical toys

Music making is great for helping children learn cause and effect, and it also helps them start to understand how their own actions impact on the environment. Make it easier on your ears by playing music you like for them to play along to.

## Interactive toys

There are so many toys on the market that provide your child with interaction, such as buttons that provide sounds or light up when pressed. Try to choose one that has an educational theme, such as animal noises, numbers or the alphabet.

# It Is Not Always Easy – Troubleshooting Tips

## 'My child is showing no interest in trying to walk'

Some children don't really show an interest in walking until they are nearly two, so try not to worry too much. Don't force a child to stand up and walk before she is ready, but do talk to your health visitor if you are concerned that there may be a medical reason for her not walking. The following ideas could help inspire even the most reluctant walker to try out her feet:

- Introduce your child to slightly older children who are already walking – children learn best by copying. Seeing other children running and jumping is almost guaranteed to have the desired effect!
- 'This Little Piggy': this traditional game (see page 22) promotes interest in a child's feet and helps her become

87

aware of the sensations of things touching her feet. This will help her adjust her balance as she stands and responds to the sensation of having her feet on the floor.

- Activity stations (a low-level table with objects or activities to play with, see page 66) encourage a child to be vertical and help her feel more steady on her feet.

- Swimming/paddling pools: kicking in water is a similar action to the stepping movement. Children naturally kick in water (a splashy bath is a substitute if you can't get to the swimming pool) so this will develop her leg muscles, giving her more confidence when it comes to standing and taking her first steps.

## 10 Fun Things to Do with Your Child

1. Take a walk and smell some of the flowers you see.
2. Build a tower to knock down.
3. Paddle in a river.
4. Make a mud pie in the garden.
5. Visit a library.
6. Pet an animal.
7. Take a bark rubbing.
8. Feed the ducks.
9. Make a photo scrapbook.
10. Blow bubbles together.

## Making Memories

What were your baby's first words?

1. ........................................................................................

2. ........................................................................................

3. ........................................................................................

When did she take her first step?

........................................................................................

Where did you go on your first trip away?

........................................................................................

........................................................................................

What is her favourite game?

........................................................................................

........................................................................................

How many parts of the body can she point at when asked?

........................................................................................

What's her favourite song?

........................................................................................

........................................................................................

**play**

## Your Notes

..................................................................................................

..................................................................................................

..................................................................................................

..................................................................................................

..................................................................................................

..................................................................................................

..................................................................................................

..................................................................................................

..................................................................................................

..................................................................................................

..................................................................................................

..................................................................................................

..................................................................................................

..................................................................................................

..................................................................................................

..................................................................................................

..................................................................................................

# Chapter Five
# Imagination
# (18–24 Months)

A toddler's world will be opening up and her brain will be developing rapidly, with connections between neurons forming at a staggering rate. Having only been in the world for a short while, children at this age do not yet understand the limitations of physics and biology – for them anything is possible. This means that young children have the most amazing imaginations but they don't realise the difference between reality and fantasy.

Parents are often quick to point out what is not possible and try to help children understand the rules of the world. While this is important, nurturing a child's innate imagination is hugely beneficial for their future development as it facilitates problem-solving, inventions and initiative and is a protective factor against mental-health issues.

It can be great fun entering your child's imaginary world. Let her lead you and try not to quash the flights of fancy with too much realism – there is plenty of time for that in later life!

Stories and imaginative games will appeal to children at this age and will promote a whole range of skills including language, concentration, social skills and problem-solving.

## What to Look Out for During this Stage

### Physical and sensory development

#### Senses

Children's senses are fully developed and may seem overly sensitive to adults. Young children's hearing is particularly acute and they have a wider range of sounds that they can hear. It is not uncommon for young children to find loud noises particularly unpleasant, and almost painful.

Children with impaired hearing will be slower to learn language and, as words are starting to emerge now, it is a common time for hearing impairments to be diagnosed. You can check your child's general level of hearing: when she is sitting up, for example in a high chair, try standing behind her, slightly to one side, and making a sudden noise such as a cough. You would expect your toddler to turn towards that side to see where the noise came from. Try this on both sides.

If you are worried, there are more detailed tests that your health visitor, GP or local children's centre will be able to help you access.

#### Movement

Muscle development is refining at this age and your child's pincer grip will be gaining strength and becoming more evident. Toddlers are now able to stack bricks and cups with relative care and stability, and may find more delicate tasks, such as threading beads on to string, possible.

Gross muscles will be gaining in strength and walking will be well established for most children, although some may still be unsteady on their feet.

Stairs and steps will become a focus and, although she will have wanted to go up them for some time, now she will want to come down too! Until your child is really confident around steps, encourage her to descend the staircase feet-first on her tummy to start with, and then on her bottom. It is always crucial to supervise and assist when she is around any stairs – she will still be unsteady, and falling is a very real possibility.

Climbing, in appropriate and safe environments, such as playgrounds, the garden, playgroups or soft play centres, will help develop your child's awareness of risk and enable her to learn to judge her own abilities, while strengthening muscles and improving her balance.

Active play (i.e. play that requires physical movement) will further develop the important muscle groups and keep her rapidly growing body strong and healthy. The British Toy and Hobby Association suggests that active play not only benefits children in terms of cardiovascular fitness but also helps to build long-term healthier lifestyles with better physical, intellectual and social skills.

Try to encourage plenty of active play – this can be walking using the support of a push-along object or, when she is confident on her feet, you can encourage running, hopping, kicking balls or catch.

Movement at this age can really help your toddler learn about her environment, exploring new places and objects. Although you don't often associate movement with thought and feelings, the two can very much complement each other. She will be thinking about her next movement, understanding what she wants to attain and working out in her own way how to achieve this. The feeling of satisfaction and success will boost her confidence and make her want to do it again.

Praising your child's achievements can build confidence further and will help her develop a desire for further progression. She will soon learn that in order to get a toy or exciting object that is out of reach she needs to walk or maybe even climb to reach it. Once she has achieved her goal she will want to do this again and again in order to reach other objects that are of interest to her.

### Coordination

As a child's coordination improves, so does her desire for independence. She may be trying to do everything without help, which – although frustrating at times for you as a parent – is crucial for her development.

Using a fork and spoon to eat is now easily achievable and, although messy to start with, will really help her coordination develop further. She will love the independence of feeding herself and it will create a sense of achievement. Brushing her teeth and hair independently and washing her own face are also great at further developing hand–eye coordination. Try doing these activities alongside your child and help her mirror your behaviour. Washing your face as she does hers, brushing your teeth together and letting her mimic your actions will really encourage her to be independent. Parents will need to 'just finish off' her teeth brushing to make sure it has been done properly.

Dressing herself will also become achievable. You can really boost your child's confidence in this by buying clothes and shoes that are easy for her to put on and take off. This will allow her to achieve more without your added help. Leggings, jogging bottoms and T-shirts are all easy to use. Shoes with Velcro will be easier for her to put on without help than those with buckles or laces. Avoid belts and other complicated fastenings that she will struggle with, as these can hinder her advances and make her feel less able. You can also give your child some choice in what she wears – see page 99 for more on this.

Your child will now be coordinating movements – kicking a football is achievable and so is jumping. Once these skills are mastered she will do them more and more. Finding activities or sports that will help her develop and progress in these areas will be great for her.

## Thinking and communication

### Thinking

Now your toddler is mobile, she is open to a vast array of experiences and can explore her environment thoroughly. This leads to an explosion in her understanding of the world, and her thinking skills are becoming increasingly sophisticated as she starts using trial-and-error learning. It is wonderful to watch a child learn a new skill and master tasks such as fitting shapes into a shape sorter or putting pieces of a large jigsaw puzzle together.

Colours, shapes and sizes are becoming interesting to her now, and, although she won't be able to recognise them yet, name repetition from you will help her to develop this recognition. She can try to sort objects into different categories with your help and she will love getting these correct.

As thinking skills develop, children gain a further understanding of more complex ideas, such as time. For example, 'Tomorrow we can go to the park', and 'Yesterday was fun'.

Children are still very much exploring and trying to make sense of the world at this age, and this is done naturally, without the need for hothousing. Playing games and communicating with

**play**

your child, telling her what you are doing and what is happening, will promote the development of thinking skills in a fun, non-pressured way.

Even at this young age, children will employ thinking skills in order to make sense of their world. Your child will be watching you and the people and events around her, picking up everyday behaviour and imitating certain actions, such as throwing away an object as rubbish or 'helping' around the house with the cleaning.

### Language

As speech is developing rapidly you will start understanding far more of what she is saying. Her vocabulary will be expanding, and she may be able to point to pictures in a book and tell you what they are.

She will understand simple requests and respond accordingly. For example, 'Can you give me the spoon?' or 'Can you clap your hands?' It is worth nothing that children will pay attention to the nouns (or concrete objects) in a sentence so they respond better to positive rather than negative instructions. Telling a child what you do want her to do is much more likely to get results than telling her what not to do. For example, if you say, 'Don't put your finger in the plug socket,' children focus on 'finger' and 'plug socket'. You are more likely to get better results if you ask your child to 'put your hands on your lap'.

When you say 'No', a child will get confused if you overexplain the reason behind this. Simple, clear communication at this age, with body language and tone of voice backing up the message, will help children understand and, in turn, will help them communicate themselves. For example, if your child wants to jump off a high wall, you can simply say, 'No, you may hurt yourself,' rather than listing several injuries she may encounter if she did this. Your child will love having books read to her and will listen intently. Rhymes and poems will help her to remember words and their meanings and she will enjoy the rhythm and repetition they offer. She may well have a 'favourite' book, wanting you to read it over and over again to her; although this may become tedious for you as the reader, it is very beneficial in developing her language and comprehension skills, so try to be as patient as possible.

If your child is not yet starting to put words together to form sentences, it will not be long until she does, and from here her communication really starts to take shape. You can try to develop her speech and the muscles used by introducing bubble blowing, with her blowing the bubbles instead of you. She will love this activity and the movements used to blow need to be strengthened for correct pronunciation.

## Social and emotional development

Her social skills and her need to interact with peers will be developing, although 'friendships' will not be formed just yet. Toddler groups, nursery and meeting up with other toddlers will all promote this interaction and encourage her communication skills further.

She may bite or hit out at someone or something that is upsetting her, hug a teddy when she is sad, or hug a peer when they have done something nice for her. She won't yet be able to describe her feelings or those of her peers but you can help her emotional development by talking about your feelings with simple words such as 'Sam made me sad today'.

It is important to start introducing boundaries and help your child to understand that 'no' means no. She will start to understand right and wrong and may start to cover up her mistakes to avoid getting into trouble.

Experiencing different environments will provide your child with new feelings, sensations and enhanced thoughts. She may act differently when playing in a garden or forest environment than when she is in a soft play centre.

Companionship can also have differing effects on her feelings and thoughts: playing alone may make her feel independent or lonely, while playing with other children can make her feel either anxious or confident. All environments are beneficial to her and will promote different senses, feelings and thoughts. She will need to learn to play by herself just as much as playing in a group, so encourage her to explore the different environments open to her as much as possible.

## Routines

Routines are important at this age; children will know their routines and may become fractious if the routines are disturbed. However, setting up strict routines can cause problems if they are not always adhered to. It is important to find a balance between having stability within their routines to give children security and promote attachment, and avoiding overly rigid routines that make it difficult for children to socialise or build relationships with other friends and family members. Try to have flexible routines so that children are more able to cope with change, and be prepared for a bit of a struggle the first couple of days after your return to the normal routine.

### Development of identity

Your child will know several body parts by now and will be able to point to them when prompted. She may even be trying to say some of the names.

Role play can be a great activity to help mould your child's understanding and development of her identity, while also making sense of the world. She will love dressing up as her favourite character – e.g. playing 'Mum' with dolls, feeding them and changing nappies (again mimicking tasks from her everyday life). Children's imagination has no limits and role play allows her to explore both real life and fantasy.

Dancing and singing is a very popular method of expressing thoughts and showing that your child is developing her own identity. She may have favourite songs and it is interesting for parents to watch their child dance to different types of music.

Performing, whether acting, singing or playing an instrument, boosts confidence and can help children cooperate with others. It can also provide a creative outlet for emotions and helps children learn to express themselves. With encouragement from an early age, children are less likely to be self-conscious or shy about performing as they get older.

### Independence

Your child is able to make simple decisions now and wants to put these into practice. Getting dressed is a common one to start with. She will now be aware of what she wants to wear and what she doesn't, and will be very determined to dress herself. This can be stressful for a carer when she takes time to achieve this task, but it is also important to encourage this new independence. Trying to leave plenty of time for her to be as independent as possible can take some of the stresses away. Some of the outfits she will put together can be very amusing and inappropriate; however, this is her learning curve and her way of creating and expressing her personal identity, so try to accept it and encourage her as much as possible.

Too much choice can be overwhelming so, while it is fun to let your child dress up in an eclectic mix of clothes during playtime, it is a good idea to give her a limited choice (e.g. a red or blue top) – this will support her development yet still enable you to get out of the door before lunchtime!

### Creative play: why is it important?

In a world where children are increasingly having to follow instructions and abide by adult-imposed rules, creative play, such as arts and crafts, den building and imaginative role play, allows children to be in control. This is really important for children as it helps them make decisions, boosts their confidence and enables them to experiment and explore ideas that they have in their incredibly fertile minds.

Creative play allows children to express themselves and develops a range of other skills in the process. Fine motor skills are developed as children manipulate their materials – placing, threading and moulding. Cognitive skills are developed in the design and planning stages of creative play, and social and emotional skills are enhanced through shared projects, as well as the act of giving the creations as gifts, which promotes attachment.

Parents can help their children engage in creative play in a number of ways:

1. Have a box of scrap materials and 'junk modelling' such as empty toilet rolls, cereal boxes and clean yoghurt pots, which can all be used creatively. Up-cycling (rather than re-cycling) is a new vogue and children can enjoy finding new creative uses for these old things around the house.

2. Buy age-appropriate arts and crafts kits as presents or rewards rather than sweets or other treats.

3. Take time to look at your child's creation and give positive feedback – comments such as 'I love that scary green dinosaur!' are much more motivating and boost self-esteem more than a generic 'That's really good'.

4.  Reward and reinforce effort and concentration –
    this will help children persevere when tasks are
    challenging and can be wonderful for self-esteem.
5.  Help your child take pride in her creation by displaying
    it and showing it to visitors in front of your child.

Creative play doesn't have to be expensive; a box of toilet
rolls, clean yoghurt pots, sticky tape, old clothes, glue and
coloured pens/paint can provide hours of entertainment.
So, before throwing rubbish away, see if it can't be kept in
the junk box and used to stimulate your children's creativity.

## Playful Activities

### Blowing bubbles

This is great fun and the blowing motion strengthens lip control
and increases breath capacity, which are both required for speech.
Jumping or chasing to pop the bubbles promotes muscle strength
and movement.

### Arts and crafts

Creativity can really start to develop around this age and simple arts
and crafts are achievable. Painting, drawing and sticking things on
paper can help to promote fine motor skills, imagination and colour
identification, as well as other senses. Although this type of play
can get messy, the skills you help your child develop are definitely
worth the clearing up. Use play mats and newspapers to protect

surfaces and make tidying away quicker and easier. If you really can't face having your house covered in glitter, there are plenty of nurseries and art groups that you can attend away from your own house where children can be creative together (and you don't have to clean up the mess).

Try to give your child lots of different textures to play with, such as material, cardboard, cotton wool, foil or dried pasta. She will love making you or a relative a nice picture for your wall.

## Self-drawing

Using a very long piece of paper (an old wallpaper roll is good for this), draw around your child and then let her colour herself in. It can be fun to do this every six months so she can see how much she has grown.

## Musical instruments

Children love to make noise – and usually the louder the better! Introduce a wide variety of musical instruments that are age-appropriate such as drums, maracas and tambourines. Your child will soon learn the sounds that each of them make and that some instruments can make different sounds depending on how you play them. For example a tambourine can be shaken to make a jingly bell noise or banged to make a drum sound.

## Drawing

Children love colouring and drawing. Allow your child to use a variety of (non-toxic and washable) pens, crayons or paints to create scribbles, marks and patterns. She will be showing signs of wanting to choose from the selection of tools to create her own picture. If you want less mess there are also 'aqua drawing/doodling' mats and pens that use water to create marks and colours that fade, and these can be just as rewarding and challenging.

### Wall 'painting'

Give your child a bucket of water and a large paintbrush and help her develop her arm muscles and creativity by 'painting' the garden wall, fence or pavement.

### Necklace threading

Using a piece of string and some dried pasta (penne works best), your child can try to make necklaces by threading the pasta on to the string. She can then paint the pasta and dip it in glitter to make it prettier.

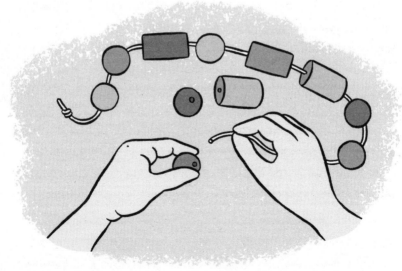

## Dressing up

Any clothes your child can find will make for great dressing up – Mummy's skirts or Daddy's shirts and ties, pirate and fairy costumes or even everything in her own wardrobe. She will have great fun trying them all on and making weird and wonderful outfits (particularly with your favourite shoes, which are far too big). Let her imagination and creativity take control. Photos of her outfits will offer great memories in years to come.

## Choosing Toys

### Shape sorter

Shape sorters are great at getting your child's brain to think, problem-solve and to learn the different shapes. They provide her with a challenge that is achievable and help her to learn through the 'trial and error' process.

### Simple jigsaw puzzles

This classic activity provides endless fun for a toddler. It will improve concentration, problems-solving skills (through working out which pieces fit together) and strengthen her fine motor skills. The satisfaction she feels when she has finished the puzzle and can see the full picture will really boost her confidence and make her want to do it again and again. Start with simple two- or three-piece puzzles to help your child learn how to join the pieces together.

**play**

## Construction toys

Building even the simplest of towers can promote many skills and abilities. Fine motor skills are strengthened, as is concentration, and there are plenty of opportunities to improve vocal skills as well as shape and colour recognition.

A child's imagination is endless and she is able to use this to create anything she likes, whether it be a house, dog or car. Once she has finished one construction she can take it apart and do another.

## Bath toys

Bath toys can bring many benefits and educational opportunities (e.g. understanding floating, sinking and how materials change when they get wet). From the traditional rubber duck and other floating animals to wall-mounted activity centres, these toys can all help make bath time not just a cleaning process but also a fun activity.

Choose toys that are age-appropriate. Animals will be exciting and she can use them to learn names and the noises they make. Boats and other floatables open her up to the concept that not everything sinks in water.

Wall-mounted activity centres often have water wheels, cups and buttons, which will utilise her fine motor skills, cognitive development and imagination.

Bath toys can be truly brilliant at making bath time less stressful and more exciting – particularly when it comes to washing her hair and face. You can use toys to help make this essential routine fun and enjoyable … distracting her from the parts she doesn't enjoy.

**Role play toys**

Children will watch your behaviour and routines and try to copy them. Toy hoovers, kitchens or workbenches really help them to mimic your world. Your child will love to hoover at the same time as you, or cook you lunch, as you do for her.

## It Is Not Always Easy – Troubleshooting Tips

### 'I'm still not getting a full night's sleep'

By this age you may have managed to solve the big issues of sleep, but it is likely that there are a few remaining trouble spots that keep you or your partner up from time to time. Bedtime issues often continue to be paramount in parents' minds long after the first year. That is because, as your child grows, you can expect bedtime difficulties to recur with almost every new stage of development. But you needn't despair – there are solutions that will leave everybody in your family happy and your toddler asleep. The trick is in helping your child learn to go to sleep herself.

How much sleep does your one- to two-year-old need? Typically, children this age sleep for about 11.5 hours at night and take two naps during the day, giving a total of about 14 hours out of every 24. By the time your child reaches her second birthday she may be sleeping about an hour less, with only one nap making up part of her typical 13 hours or so of downtime. However, you need not be concerned if your little one doesn't exactly fit this pattern, as long as both you and your child feel well rested; normal sleep requirements vary greatly from child to child.

Don't get frustrated in your crusade to help your child sleep through the night. Almost no one, parent or child, ever really sleeps through the whole night without waking. Think about it for a moment – don't you sometimes wake? Don't you go to the bathroom or fluff your pillow or prod your snoring spouse?

Much the same is true for your child, who often will wake up briefly during the night – as she goes through the normal cycles of deep and light sleep, as a noisy truck goes by or as she finds herself in an uncomfortable position. Your goal should be to help your child fall asleep when it's bedtime and return to sleep easily – and by herself – when she wakes during the night. If she doesn't know how to do this, her only recourse will be to cry out to you to help her get back to sleep.

Here are some tips on getting her to settle:

- Make sure the room is dark and at the correct temperature (approximately 18°C/65°F).
- Make sure there aren't too many things in the cot for her to play with. (A comfort toy or blanket is fine, especially one that has your scent on it.)
- Don't go in to check on her too quickly. Listen to the crying and then trust your instinct – parents are remarkably adept at distinguishing between different types of crying.

### 'My child gets very upset whenever I leave her'

At some point during their development, all children will experience separation anxiety. It is very common and completely normal. However, it can be difficult for parents to cope with a baby or toddler who gets panicky and upset when they are not around. The good news is that, for the vast majority of children, separation anxiety happens in phases and will not last forever.

It often starts at around eight months and usually subsides as your baby nears one year old or a few months after. However, it may come back with a vengeance around two years, once your toddler becomes aware of her own independence.

Your toddler will learn – through the responsiveness of those close to her – to recognise the patterns of your comings and goings in her daily life, and when there really is something to be upset about. However, this is not something she learns overnight.

The best way to deal with separation anxiety is to give your child reassurance – over and over again – that your absence doesn't mean that you have gone away forever. Even if your toddler's distress is upsetting you, it is not necessary to give up plans to go out or return to work. It is part of her emotional growth to learn that others can care for her as well and she can trust you to come back soon.

Patience, understanding and calm reassurance are the main responses you can use to handle separation anxiety. Other common strategies include doing the following:

- Wave bye-bye when you leave: It's a simple tactic but one that many parents ignore. If your child thinks you might disappear at any given moment without notice, she is not going to let you out of her sight.

- Stay calm: Try to stay calm and positive – even if she is hysterical. Talk to her evenly and reassure her that you will be back soon. To keep the situation light, try adopting a silly parting phrase such as, 'See you later, alligator,' or your own made-up alternative. Getting your child in the habit of responding with, 'In a while, crocodile,' will also help serve as a distraction.

- Use a comfort object: Having a reminder of Mum or Dad may help your toddler cope in your absence, so when you go out, leave her with a source of comfort. A security object – a blanket, a stuffed animal or even her very own thumb – can also be a source of solace, and a soft material object that has a familiar smell can be a very powerful comforter, so don't wash her favourite blanket/cuddly toy just before a period of absence.

• Leave at the same time: Goodbyes are always easier when it is your child who does the exiting. Instead of you leaving her behind, have the babysitter take her for a quick trip to the park or out for a stroll as you head out the door. Make sure your child understands that you are going out as well. Otherwise she will be doubly upset when she returns to find the house empty.

• Involve her in an activity: Allow your toddler and her caregiver to get engrossed in an activity before you leave. When the time comes for you to go, give your child a quick kiss goodbye and make a beeline for the door. She may still cry, but the activity can serve as a distraction soon after your departure.

• Let her learn to cope: No parent wants their child to feel any unnecessary sadness, but coping with separation is one of the many stresses your child will have to learn to manage in life. Sometimes doing nothing – especially if you've already tried everything – is the best advice. If your child's clinginess is so severe that you can't even cross the room without a protest, for example, you may be making the situation worse by constantly caving in to her demands. If you know that she is safe, it is okay to let her cry a bit. In a matter-of-fact voice, reassure her that everything is okay, then go ahead and do whatever it is you need to do – without feeling guilty.

## 10 Fun Things to Do with Your Child

1. Take her sledging.
2. Let her hold a friendly guinea pig or rabbit.
3. Make a bird feeder and hang it in your garden.
4. Let her roll down a steep hill on her side.
5. Go for a walk in the rain with her mac and wellies on.
6. Make a wish in a wishing well.
7. Take her for a donkey ride on a beach.
8. Find a rainbow together.
9. Build a sandcastle.
10. Search for fairies and elves living under toadstools in the forest.

## Making Memories

What is your child's favourite story/character?

.........................................................................................................

.........................................................................................................

When did you first notice your child concentrating on something?

.........................................................................................................

Where is your favourite outdoor place to go with your toddler?

.........................................................................................................

.........................................................................................................

.........................................................................................................

What sort of music does your toddler like listening to the most?

..............................................................................................

..............................................................................................

What is your child's favourite toy?

..............................................................................................

What is your child's favourite dressing-up outfit?

..............................................................................................

Are there any areas of development that you're concerned about at this stage?

..............................................................................................

..............................................................................................

..............................................................................................

## Your Notes

..............................................................................................

..............................................................................................

..............................................................................................

..............................................................................................

..............................................................................................

..............................................................................................

..............................................................................................

..............................................................................................

..............................................................................................

..............................................................................................

..............................................................................................

..............................................................................................

..............................................................................................

..............................................................................................

..............................................................................................

..............................................................................................

..............................................................................................

# Chapter Six
# Language
# (2–3 Years)

Children learn to talk at different ages, but by their second birthday most will have up to 300 words in their vocabulary. Words become more comprehensible, with clear speech being evident most of the time. Your child will now also be linking some words together, often between two and four words, in order to form basic sentences, while gaining a real sense of the meanings of words by starting to use the correct word in the appropriate situation.

As your child develops she will learn some of the names of her peers and will be able to call them using their names (even if she can't pronounce all the sounds correctly). Playing with others is also more possible now and will promote further communication, although many children will still play in parallel rather than interacting with the other children's part of play.

Of course, communication skills are so much more than just words, and both verbal and non-verbal components are required as well as the ability to both give and receive communications. Your child will also need to understand the social function of language and know when to speak. As it is what most people do naturally, the best thing you can do to promote your child's communication is to involve her in yours. This is why family mealtimes and joint play activities are so beneficial. Children watch, learn and copy their parents' communication styles, so the more you include your child in conversation – however simple and age-appropriate the questions and comments – the more confident she will be at communicating with others.

Be warned, however, that frustrations are very common at this age as a child's thought process is often far more advanced than her language skills, resulting in frequent toddler tantrums. This can be a stressful time for all so try to encourage your toddler's use of language by making her learn how to ask for the things she wants, rather than pre-empting her every need.

Your child can now point to an object when asked and will have a much wider understanding of the names of objects within her environment. Usually this comes first, followed by learning to use verbs, but, equally, there are some adjectives (e.g. colours) that your child may learn early on (along with the word 'no'!) Towards the age of three she will be able to name other things she sees in books, for example animals, modes of transport or items around the house.

## What to Look Out for During this Stage

### Physical and sensory development

#### *Movement*

Your child's muscles will be rapidly developing and gaining in strength at this age, and all the movements she has been learning between one and two will now be easily achievable. Running will be fun and, although she may be a little unsteady, she will enjoy this newfound freedom and speed.

She may also be attempting to use alternate feet when climbing shallow stairs, rather than ascending one foot at a time, and, although she may still need supervising, she will be increasingly capable of doing this independently. You may notice an improvement in her balance as she becomes more stable on her feet. She may even be able to stand on one leg for a few seconds – this is a great exercise for balance and coordination and should be encouraged on each leg.

Jumping is a newly developed skill. During this stage your child will develop leg muscle strength that will allow her to jump and land more confidently. She will enjoy jumping off low-level objects, and this is something else you should encourage as long as she is supervised. Children have a natural fear of heights and falling, and so won't intentionally jump from an object that is too high for them. However, at this age they are not yet able to accurately assess risk and may well get themselves into dangerous situations (another feature of the 'eyes-in-the-back-of-your-head' stage).

### Food and drink

Your child is now capable of eating the same food as the rest of the family, if she isn't already doing so. However, this is the time where she can show fussiness and where bad food habits can be easily formed.

Family meals are really beneficial and should be prioritised when possible. They work best when they are enjoyable for everyone. Try getting your child involved in as much of the food preparation as possible, from washing potatoes to finding her own plate and mug.

Although she will have probably tried a range of foods by now, it is still a learning curve for her and the more variety, textures, colours and tastes you introduce to her – and she sees you eating – the better. This doesn't mean you have to cook whole meals from scratch every day; simple meals can be equally as nutritious as elaborate ones and you may enjoy the mealtimes more if you have not spent ages in the kitchen preparing a meal that your toddler may well knock on to the floor, refuse to eat or spill over herself. One useful idea is to always make too much and freeze a few portions. You can defrost and re-heat it on a day when you have limited time to cook something from fresh.

Remember that your child's stomach is far smaller than yours and so she will need much smaller portions. Try not to overfeed your child; take her lead to determine when she is full. To help mealtimes go smoothly, avoid giving your child anything to eat for at least 45 minutes before a meal. If she seems hungry, give her a glass of water, as she is unable to distinguish between the sensations of hunger and thirst at this age and water will not fill her up or put her off her meal.

Children of this age can still be very messy eaters and, although this can be a trying time for you, it can be very beneficial for your toddler if you allow her to continue to explore her food through touch and play. (Protecting the area around and underneath your child will make clearing up easier, and eating outside in the summer is great for everyone.)

Encourage your child to take an interest in food through imaginary play. It can be really useful to invest in a pretend kitchen with plastic food to help with this. Familiarise her with the different food names and popular dishes you cook. Play restaurants, ordering and eating food and encourage her to prepare dinner for her favourite toy and feed it, whether it is a dinosaur or doll. This play idea can also be particularly useful if you have a really fussy eater as it can create an interest in food.

### Coordination

As your child's coordination is developing she is now able to take part in more complex activities, such as building a tower out of bricks (the number of bricks she chooses to use will grow as she gets older).

Drawing with a crayon or paintbrush will have more definition and shape. Rather than a scribble, she will be drawing straight vertical lines, and towards the end of this year she will be attempting to draw circles. With these two new skills, a person can be drawn simply (with a circle for the head and lines for the body, legs and arms), and you can encourage this creativity by displaying her artwork somewhere prominent and pointing it out to other members of the family.

### Teething

Your child will probably cut her last few teeth between the ages of two and three. These are her 'second molars', although don't be alarmed if they are still not through before three as it is not uncommon for them to appear later. Unfortunately this is painful and can cause more sleepless nights, although it shouldn't last for too long (approximately two days per tooth).

## Thinking and communication

In addition to the explosion of language that occurs during this year, your child will be developing her thinking skills, which will also increase her ability to communicate.

Children are learning to label and then to categorise at this stage. As we touched upon earlier, one of the most common categories that children learn first is colour, and your child may be able to 'find all the red ones' when you ask her to – this is the first sign of her developing ability to categorise.

Until around the age of two, children need very simple, step-by-step instructions. As they enter their third year they are able to follow more complex commands, possibly with three separate components – parents at this stage often report being surprised by how much their child understands compared with what they are able to say.

Children are starting to understand prepositions of place – such as 'on', 'over', 'next to', etc. – and may be able to follow complex commands such as, 'Put the bowl on the table next to the cup.'

Your toddler will be beginning to understand abstract concepts like 'sooner' and 'later', but will respond better to time references that can be pinned on something concrete. For example, 'We are going to the shops and then we are going to see Granny for tea. After tea we will go home and have a bath,' is easier to understand than more abstract concepts of time such as 'later on' or 'tomorrow'.

## Social and emotional development

### Development of identity

At around two and a half, as your child is starting to become more aware of her peers and the people around her, she will start recognising the difference between girls and boys – known as the development of gender identity – and will increasingly identify herself in the correct gender.

It is not uncommon for young children to mix up genders – a boy may say he wants to be a mummy when he grows up, or a girl may want to be a daddy. As gender identity develops, your child will learn the difference and often identify more with the parent of the same gender. When this happens, a boy may refuse to wear or play with anything considered to be 'girly' and a girl may decide she only likes pink, or wants to dress up and play with make-up.

There is a big debate around the extent to which the gender stereotyping is socially constructed and how much is due to the fact that girls and boys are biologically different (see page 125). Encourage your child to develop her own identity and support her interest in a range of activities, regardless of the gender stereotypes present.

Your child may want to choose more of her own clothes. This will help her develop her own identity further and express her likes and dislikes through her choice of colours, styles and textures.

She will still have a strong interest in herself and often talk about her body and what she has done recently. This is all about her learning who she is, as well as letting you know. As she moves towards her third birthday she will be able to accurately name several body parts and point to them when asked. Songs such as 'Head, Shoulders, Knees and Toes' (see page 198) are good for helping those children who may be struggling with learning their body parts.

As your child is starting to learn new words she is able to express feelings and thoughts in a far more complex way, allowing others to understand her and become aware of her personal thoughts. Letting her choose activities that she wants to take part in enables her to establish further her likes and dislikes.

### Independence

Your little one will now really enjoy being self-sufficient and will have now developed the 'can do' attitude. She will want to zip up her coat, get herself dressed and attempt her buttons all by herself. These are all possible at this stage as her pincer grip is well developed now, but these skills take practice (it can be a long wait if you are trying to get out of the door!) Although this is very frustrating at the time, it is worth persevering with as it promotes independence and boosts confidence (plus you don't want to be the only parent still doing up a zip for your 10-year-old). Try allowing an extra 10 minutes for your toddler to get herself ready.

She may also want to brush her own teeth all by herself. Her coordination is advanced enough to enable her to do a rough brush but not the thorough brush that is needed. Make sure you go over the teeth afterwards as poor dental hygiene can cause weaker adult teeth and painful visits to the dentist later on. If your toddler won't allow you to go over her teeth after she has brushed them, create games to help it become fun. Line up a few teddies and ask her to help brush their teeth. As she is doing theirs you can try to do hers so you can all check each other's teeth. Allow her to go over your teeth to make sure you have done yours properly too.

### Attachment

Children are normally securely attached to several caregivers by the age of three but may still have one or two that they seek out in times of distress. They will become less clingy over this year but may seem to regress with bouts of clinginess when they are ill, tired or anxious.

## Playful Activities

### Role play

Role play can take many forms. The use of play food encourages your child to pretend to cook dinner and to feed 'teddy' or 'dolly'. Give her a spoon and a bowl to hold and ask her to feed the toys. She will love to pretend her teddy has eaten all of his dinner and will imitate your movements from when you have fed her. (This can be an added help at dinner time, as mentioned on page 83, as you can encourage her to eat the food using the 'one mouthful for teddy and one mouthful for you' technique.)

## Balls

Playing with balls is great fun for this age group and provides valuable exercise for your child. Once your child has mastered rolling a ball, she will start wanting to throw it underarm. Towards three years she will start trying to catch large balls using outstretched arms, although this will be a difficult skill to perfect and she will need plenty of practice. Kicking a ball in a certain direction is gradually getting better and aiming for targets will help your child improve her control over where the ball lands. Games involving running after balls promote fitness and healthy activity levels.

## Matching games

With her new colour-labelling skills, try making the job of sorting the laundry into a game. You can ask your child to find the blue socks, for example, and then see if she can match them into pairs.

## Bug hunts

Children are curious about their surroundings, and letting them explore under stones and finding spiders in cupboards will help them not become squeamish as they get older. Go on a bug hunt and try collecting leaves and twigs in a jam jar and popping any creepy-crawlies you find in there too (remember to put the lid on, but have air holes in it or the bugs won't survive very long!)

**play**

### Scissor play

As your child's hand–eye coordination develops she is able to use scissors to do simple cutting, which will aid her pincer grip and fine motor skills. She will be expected to be able to use scissors by the time she has started school at least, so it is a good time to start introducing them. Make sure the scissors have blunt ends and are child-friendly to avoid accidents and injuries; there are plenty on the market that only cut paper and not skin, hair or clothes.

### Memory game

Choose three or four objects from around the house and ask your child to look at them and remember them for 10 seconds, then hide her eyes. When she can't see, take one away and hide it behind your back. She can now look again and has to work out which one you have taken. If she does this easily you can add more objects.

### 'What's the word?'

Tell your child a familiar story or rhyme but miss words out. For example, 'Jack and Jill went up the hill to fetch a pail of …?' Get her to fill in the missing word. This can be a great game for the car on long journeys and promotes listening skills.

### Lolly making

Using fresh fruit juice, fill up ice-lolly moulds together. (Doing this over the sink will keep mess to a minimum.) Place the filled moulds in the freezer and wait for the lollies to freeze. This activity will teach your child how liquid freezes when it gets very, very cold. It will also help her hand–eye coordination as she pours the juice into the moulds and provide her with some healthy desserts.

## Toys for girls and boys

The debate on whether the difference in toy choices is innate or socially constructed rages on.

In 2002 psychologist Dr Gerianne Alexander of Texas A&M University and Professor Melissa Hines of City University, London, ran an experiment using both gender-specific toys, gender-neutral toys and 44 male and 44 female vervet monkeys.[4] Throughout the research they watched and monitored the monkeys' play preferences, and they found that male monkeys showed a significantly greater interest in the police car and ball, and the female monkeys showed significantly more interest in the soft doll and cooking pot. The gender-neutral toys (a picture book and a stuffed dog) were played with equally by both genders.

These findings suggest that what dictates a 'girls' toy' and 'boys' toy' is not necessarily society and our ideologies but has its roots in biological differences between girls and boys.

However, whether toy choices are truly innate or not, does it matter? As long as both genders get the opportunities to develop their full potential, should we mind whether they play with Barbie or Thomas the Tank Engine?

It is well documented that boys generally develop social skills more slowly than girls. This puts them at a significant disadvantage as they enter formal education. It is therefore worth looking for toys that encourage social development for boys.

Role play is very sociable and develops skills such as imagination, communication and cooperation, but most role play is biased towards more perceived feminine activities (mummies and daddies, etc.). However, there are toys that might help boys engage with this traditionally 'girly' type of play. Farm toys (see page 159) and military role-play products are likely to be beneficial in helping boys to play cooperatively and develop the social skills that will level the playing field for them at school. The problem lies in whether parents, teachers and childcare workers are willing to allow the boys to play with these toys in their own (often energetic and sometimes aggressive) ways in order to enable them to develop the social skills that this type of play facilitates.

Another area of imbalance is in the number of girls entering science- and mathematics-based careers. As with the role play and social development, this is a combination of both nature and nurture, but if parents ensure their daughters have access to, and engage with, construction/strategy toys there might be less of a gender division here too.

Again, there are toys that challenge the stereotypes, for example, pink sparkly construction toys, like Lego and Geomag, and science kits to make cosmetics and bubble baths. These all help girls develop an interest in science and maths and can potentially help keep their options open for future careers.

It is worth making sure children have access to non-gender-stereotyped toys, such as ride-ons, skittles or building blocks, to see how children play with them and whether they help balance out the play opportunities for the genders.

## Choosing Toys

Peer pressure is still a relatively minor influence on children of this age and parents have the biggest say in which toys children have access to in this age group. However, children do make their preferences known and, especially if they have older siblings, they will often aspire to have toys which make them feel more 'grown up'.

Parents are often guilty of overestimating their children's ability and intelligence and will often buy toys which are too advanced for their child. However, children's abilities and experiences vary enormously in this age group and this makes it difficult to put specific age guidelines on toys (except for on a safety basis). For example, some preschool children are able to complete complex jigsaw puzzles with more than 30 pieces, whereas others, who have not had a lot of experience with jigsaws, may struggle with the concept of fitting the pieces together and matching the colours, etc., and thus be unable to do even a four-piece puzzle without help.

When choosing toys for your child it is important to be realistic about her abilities and let her progress at her own pace. Providing her with something that is too advanced can knock her confidence and cause frustrations, yet something too easy will cause her to get bored quickly and will not offer the challenges that she needs.

Social development is considered to be the most important area of development for preschool children, so toys which encourage social interaction and skills such as sharing, turn-taking and communication are really good for this age group.

## Pull-alongs

As walking is a relativity new concept to your child, she will not get bored with dragging toys around, especially if they make a noise when they move or flap their feet. These are easy toys to take out and about too – walking a duck pull-along toy around the park can offer your child plenty of entertainment while she gets excellent exercise and strengthens her leg muscles.

## Matching pairs

As children start to learn their colours and shapes, toys and games that encourage matching pairs, such as 'memory card games', will engage your child and reinforce the skills she is learning, as well as promoting problem-solving and perseverance.

## Water or sand tables

These activity tables help develop core stability as children are moving their arms and need to stay upright in order to play. They are also good for introducing other children into your child's play activities and allowing her to play independently while gradually learning to share. Playing with water or sand is also great for developing the muscles in the hands and will promote fine motor skills.

## Simple jigsaw puzzles

Puzzles further increase hand–eye coordination, as children need to work out where pieces go and may need to turn or twist a piece to fit it into the correct place. Once your child has grasped how puzzles work, increase the number of pieces and help her to develop logical thought by matching colours to try to find the correct piece.

## Construction toys

These toys can be more complex but children can be encouraged to name the colours and start to create patterns. Helping your child to build a tower with a red layer and then a blue layer of bricks is teaching a child about colours, patterns and balance – those are some basic principles of maths and physics before she is even three!

### Favourite character toy

Children at this age often have a favourite story or television programme, and using this favourite imaginary world as a starting point for choosing toys is great, but do make sure the toys you buy are good toys in their own right and are not just popular because of the characters they are associated with.

## It Is Not Always Easy – Troubleshooting Tips

### 'My child keeps throwing tantrums'

Throwing tantrums is part of a child's development, and learning how to calm themselves and control their emotions is an important skill. Children at this age have a desire for independence and often get frustrated at not being able to understand or do something. Tantrums may also be a sign of wanting attention or a way of showing emotional overload.

Preventing a tantrum is always the best option, and establishing a few clear ground rules and sticking to them will reduce frustration as children learn the boundaries of acceptable behaviour. Tantrums are often caused when you are asking your child to do something she doesn't want to do. Turning the task into a game or play activity will often have a very different outcome.

Rather than simply asking your toddler to 'tidy her mess away', say, 'How many toys can you put in the box in 30 seconds?' She will be keen to see how many she can achieve and will be super quick at tidying away. You can also time her to see how quickly she can get her shoes on – instead of just telling her to put them on.

Children love stories and will love to hear a made-up story of your own. Use the story to entice your child into doing tasks. For example, if she refuses to brush her teeth before bedtime, suggest you tell her the story all about the little girl who refused to brush her teeth. Sitting her on your lap, tell her all about how: 'Once there was a little girl called Jessica who refused to brush her teeth …' Be as inventive as possible and your child will soon be letting you brush her teeth as she listens away to your story, especially when you get to the part about Jessica's teeth turning black and the tooth fairy not wanting them.

Positive reinforcement is a good tool for tantrum prevention, as is distraction, but these only work if the tantrum is caught before it really gets going.

Getting to the cause of the problem before a tantrum occurs is ideal but if it is too late, calmly removing the child from the rest of the group is key to avoiding exacerbating the problem. This also gives your child the opportunity to calm down without the subject of the tantrum prolonging the episode.

Children are very perceptive of adults' emotions. Staying calm will enable your child to see that her tantrum is not working and eventually learn that there are better ways to behave.

With preschool children it is also important that after a dispute they restore the troubled relationship, as they may not mean to harm others and are unaware of the consequences.

It is important to make sure that any issues have been resolved before the next playtime – that your child understands why you are upset with her behaviour and you know why she became upset. Talk to her using simple age-appropriate words and get to the root cause of the tantrum in order to pre-empt and prevent future outbreaks.

### 'My child has started biting'

Biting another child is one of the more unacceptable, aggressive behaviours in our society. The parent of the child who has been bitten is usually upset and worried about the risk of infection. If biting happens in a day-care setting, the other parents may want the biter to be expelled. Adults tend to forget that some biting is to be expected at this stage.

Children usually discover biting by chance when they are about a year old and teething. Most children first learn to bite by biting their parents in a playful manner. The biting often continues because the child considers it a game to get attention.

Later, children may bite when they are frustrated and want something from another child. At an age when children have minimal verbal skills, they may use biting as a primitive form of communication. Only later, when a child is in school, does biting become a deliberate way to express anger and intimidate others.

### *Recommendations*

1. Establish a rule: 'We never bite people.' Explain to your child that biting hurts.
2. Tell your child that if she wants something she should come to you or the carer present and ask for help or point to it. She should not bite the person who has it. If your child bites when she is angry, tell her, 'If you are upset, come and tell me, don't bite anyone.'
3. Interrupt biting with a sharp 'No'. Be sure to use an unfriendly voice and look your child straight in the eye.
4. Try to distract her when she looks as if she might bite someone before she actually does it.

### Prevention

The best time to prevent biting behaviour from becoming a habit is when the biting first starts. Be sure that no one laughs when your child bites and that no one, including older siblings, treats biting as a game. Also never give in to your child's demands because of biting. Make sure that anyone else looking after your child understands your approach and is willing to follow it.

### 'My child has become very defiant and disobedient'

Dealing with a defiant two-year-old is a notoriously difficult part of child-rearing. (They don't call it the 'terrible twos' for nothing!) When your child shouts 'No!' or hurls herself on the ground, kicking and screaming, it is no fun for you, but it is a normal reaction for a child of this age. Children crave attention and sometimes they learn that defiance gets them noticed more than good behaviour.

When your child screams and cries because she doesn't want to leave the playground, give her a hug and tell her you know it's hard to go home when she is having so much fun. The idea is to show her that, instead of being part of the problem, you are actually on her side.

Try not to get angry, even if you feel embarrassed in front of the other parents. Be kind but firm about making her leave when it is time to go. Your instinct may be to reprimand your child when her behaviour is unacceptable, but by drawing attention to bad behaviour in children at this age, we are simply amplifying it in the child's mind and therefore making it more likely that the behaviour will be repeated. This doesn't mean you should condone bad behaviour, simply say no and carry on. Speak calmly, clearly and firmly and then quickly divert your attention (and your child's, hopefully) to something more pleasant.

There is no doubt that with children you get more of what you pay attention to, so try paying lots of attention to good behaviour and less to the bad. Using reward charts effectively can really help children get out of negative behaviour patterns. Choose rewards that are motivating to your child. Try to avoid money, or too many sweets or toys. Try easy, low-cost rewards, like an extra story at bedtime, a trip to the park, a sticker or having a friend over for tea and at this age 'little and often' is the best rule as children won't yet have the ability/patience to wait for rewards.

Write the goal or goals on your incentive charts and use pictures where possible, as they are a good way to help pre-reading children understand and remember the goals as well as serving as a motivator.

Post your incentive charts in a prominent location where your child will see them often, such as the kitchen, since that is the place where most families spend a lot of time. Seeing her incentive charts may be an added motivator for your child. Remind her frequently about her incentive charts and use them consistently; being consistent when it comes to behaviour in children is really important.

## 10 Fun Things to Do with Your Child

1. Collect conkers.
2. Let her jump in muddy puddles.
3. Collect some frogspawn and look after it at home together, watching the tadpoles grow into frogs.
4. Take her fishing in a stream with a net.
5. Watch some fireworks.
6. Pick some flowers and dry them in a flower press.
7. Make a cake or some biscuits together.

8. Have fun with a disposable camera ... let her take pictures of what she likes.
9. Make a house out of a cardboard box.
10. Paint a giant picture.

## Making Memories

What is your child's favourite:

- Story? .........................................................................................
- TV programme? ...........................................................................
- Toy? ............................................................................................
- Food? ..........................................................................................
- Song? ..........................................................................................

Where was the most embarrassing place your child had a temper tantrum? What would/could you have done differently if you could replay the whole thing?

.............................................................................................................

.............................................................................................................

.............................................................................................................

.............................................................................................................

What are your child's most common phrases?

.............................................................................................................

.............................................................................................................

.............................................................................................................

.............................................................................................................

**play**

Who or what does your child talk about most?

..................................................................................................

## Your Notes

..................................................................................................

..................................................................................................

..................................................................................................

..................................................................................................

..................................................................................................

..................................................................................................

..................................................................................................

..................................................................................................

..................................................................................................

..................................................................................................

..................................................................................................

..................................................................................................

..................................................................................................

..................................................................................................

..................................................................................................

..................................................................................................

..................................................................................................

..................................................................................................

# Chapter Seven
# Social Development
# (3–4 Years)

As children enter their fourth year, they start to interact purposefully with other children. Communication is now a strong feature of a child's development, and skills such as cooperation and turn-taking become an increasingly important part of their play with others.

Helping children develop social skills is one of the most valuable things a parent can do to prepare a child for school. Those who start school being able to share and take turns while interacting and making friends with other children will not only settle into school better, they will be able to learn from their peers too. In a large class children only get a fraction of the teacher's individual attention, so being able to learn from, and work with, other children gives them a huge advantage. Starting to focus on this now gives you plenty of time to help your child develop key social skills.

## Playing with Friends

Your child will now be starting to play cooperatively with other children, and this will boost her self-esteem as she realises she is able to cope without your support. Turn-taking, sharing and teamwork are all realistically achievable now, and she can start to show compassion to others. However, be aware these skills don't develop in a single step (!), so don't be surprised if your child shares well one day but doesn't the next. Make sure you give lots of positive attention to your child when she does share. (All children develop these abilities at very different rates and such skills may occur later in many children.)

Siblings playing together can aid the understanding of turn-taking games. Try to leave children to play with their siblings or friends, rather than always being on hand to supervise and facilitate play – this will promote the social skills they require when starting school or attending preschool. So-called 'helicopter parenting' does far from help children – it instead prevents them from developing key skills, as children will naturally turn to an adult to resolve conflict or help with any challenges, and so will miss out on the opportunity to develop skills such as problem-solving, negotiation and perseverance.

## What to Look Out for During this Stage

### Physical and sensory development

#### *Movement*
A lot of behavioural issues that commonly emerge around this age (especially at bed- and mealtimes) can be managed and improved by increasing activity levels and the amount of opportunities for free play.

Outdoor play is hugely beneficial for all ages, but your older toddler will now love having the ability to explore the mud, stones and even insects, which are fascinating for this age group. She should be able to climb small structures, run, walk up and down stairs and participate in plenty of activities, which will keep her busy while building and strengthening all muscle groups.

She will now be far more in control of her own movements and start to make increasingly more complex moves. Joining different movements together to form a sequence will become achievable – for example, playing 'hopscotch' (putting a hop and jump together to travel across marked squares on the ground) or doing a simple dance routine that entertains an audience is within her reach (see page 99).

Your child will now be using movement as a regular part of her play, and as interaction with her peers is increasing she will love to incorporate this type of play with them – running, jumping and chasing. Observing peers' movements will also encourage her to try new things. For example, if she sees a friend jumping along the floor on both feet she will also want to try this, especially if they can do it together.

Being out and about can be made easier and quicker for you if she is cycling rather than walking. The benefits to her of improved balance, cardio fitness and muscle development from being on her balance bike or tricycle are far greater than sitting still in a buggy.

### Coordination

Greater gross motor skills have now developed but your child will be gaining in strength rapidly. She will be able to stand on one foot (if only for a brief amount of time) and towards four years old may start to hop, kick a large ball, throw overhand and play catch with a large ball. Catching will still be a relatively difficult concept, although some children with advanced hand–eye coordination may be able to achieve this. All these skills will become easier and more precise as she gets older.

'Practice makes perfect' is a brilliant phrase to remember with your child, as the more she does something, the quicker she will grasp it. However, remember to make activities fun and not to push her or she will be less likely to do it voluntarily. Try simplifying activities: if you find she can't catch a ball easily, try using a balloon; they are much slower so she will have more time to catch it, and they are often bigger and easier to grip too.

Dancing is now a very popular activity and she will love bopping around to her favourite songs, so this is a good time to try to encourage large movements of her arms and legs, jumping and balancing. These will all help to develop her coordination and balance skills further.

Your child's fine motor control is now sufficient for her to enjoy basic model-making and artistic activities, which require large hand and arm movements. Hand printing and colouring on large areas are easily achievable and she will love creating a picture. Her imagination is endless and she will often come up with some amazing interpretations of animals and humans!

## Thinking and communication

### Language

As we touched on in earlier stages, there is more to communication than learning to talk. Language has a wide range of purposes and once the words have been mastered children will learn to use speech to negotiate, express themselves, question, compromise, object and reassure. Your child will use all of these to articulate her personal opinions and feelings, showing the world who she is and expressing her personal values.

Having a conversation with herself and possibly having an imaginary friend can be common around this period and is perfectly normal. Many children will play imaginary games, perhaps inventing characters that don't exist or interacting with stuffed toys and dolls. Try not to dismiss imaginary friends; instead ask your child questions about him/her: 'Who is he/she?', 'What does he/she look like?', etc. It should not be a problem unless this 'friend' starts demanding things or your child starts adopting a disruptive manner due to the 'friend's' behaviour.

Your child may be using language to ask questions as part of her increasingly sophisticated thinking skills. 'Why?' can be a more than frequently used word and, although this may be frustrating after a while, it is a vital part of your child's learning and understanding of the world. Stay patient and answer her as often as you can but don't feel obliged to answer every question in huge detail. Short, simple answers are the best and fit with your child's cognitive ability and concentration span, so are more effective and memorable for her.

---

### Balancing your child's 'play diet'

The social aspect of communication cannot be overstated. While children can learn a lot about language via digital activities such as apps and computer games, these do not have the social element that person-to-person interactions involve. Computers don't change their tone of voice, nor do they put communications in context, build on shared knowledge or use body language to reinforce or add subtleties to communications. It is vital for future friendships and mental health that children communicate

---

with other people face-to-face, especially while they are learning the intricacies of human interactions.

Many people place a time limit on their child's screen time and, although this can be useful at restricting your child from sitting in front of a screen for hours, it is not always necessary if your child receives a well-balanced diet of play.

The 'Play Diet' is a practical approach to providing your children with a balanced variety of activities. Moderation in everything might sound like a boring old mantra, and something that your parents used to say, but in the same way that nutrition is about balancing the food groups, a healthy play diet is about balancing different types of play and helping parents gauge activities they want to encourage their children to participate in.

At the top of the play diet sits active free play (see page 143) and imaginative play, which should be the main source of play for your child. Next comes team games, board games, construction, reading and creative play; followed by educational toys and games. Passive screen time should provide the smallest amount of entertainment as part of a healthy play diet.

By developing a balanced approach to play and creating healthy habits as the norm, parents are able to treat children occasionally and not feel bad when, at times, they let them have more screen time than they intended. There is a lot of pressure on parents regarding the amount of screen time children have or should be allowed. It can be a little demoralising to listen to

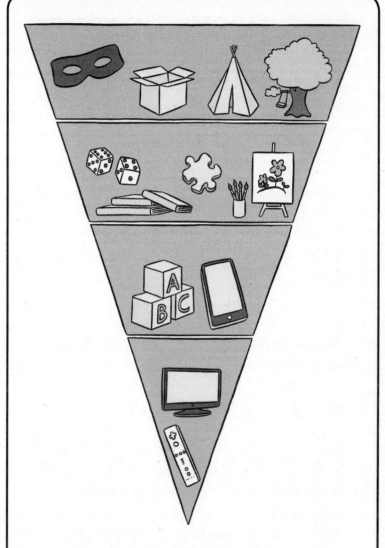

parents whose children only watch half an hour of TV at weekends, and only educational programmes at that. Of course, allowing children to sit in front of the computer, iPad or TV for hours on end isn't healthy at all but, as with everything, there is a balance. The benefits of giving children some downtime in front of the TV or iPad, where they are not putting themselves in danger or making a mess (and giving a harassed parent a few minutes to regroup!), is likely to outweigh any negative effects the TV has.

A good rule of thumb is that children are only able to concentrate for approximately 10 minutes for every year of their life so far – for example, a three-year-old can learn for 30 minutes at a time. So after this time, even educational TV or apps will have limited benefits for your child. Here are five tips to help balance your child's play diet:

- Active, child-led play is the superfood of the play diet, so try to make this a big part of your daily routine.
- Balance indoor and outdoor activities, choosing toys that can be used both inside and outside to promote active play even when it is raining – e.g. ride-ons, pop-up tents, small trampolines or a small water/sand table.
- Don't forbid screen time or tech play. Engage with it but don't use it as a babysitter.
- Mix and match playmates. Children play differently with different people so involve other family members and older and younger children, as well as peers.
- Do your research. Before buying toys, technology or apps for your child, make sure she is going to get maximum benefit from them and that they are age-appropriate.

### Thinking

By now your child's attention is sufficiently developed to enable the mastery of simple activities, which in turn boosts her confidence and the ambition needed to explore further new tasks. If your child struggles with concentration, keep games and activities quick and exciting in order to maintain her attention. The time spent on activities can be gradually increased to improve her attention span, but try to be led by her and, if she seems engrossed in an activity, where possible it is beneficial for her to be able to persevere with it.

Problem-solving is more achievable as your child will be learning, through her trial-and-error logic, to attempt to solve problems using more than one technique. When faced with a difficulty, rather than calling for an adult, it is really beneficial for your child's cognitive development and independence if she is motivated to resolve it alone. Parents can encourage this by not being too quick to jump in and do things for their child. For example, if your child gets a push-along toy stuck, encourage her to think of the different solutions, talk through various methods that may work and ask her to decide which one she believes is best. There will be many difficulties that children of this age will need an adult to sort out for them but parents are often surprised at how resourceful their young children can be, and the 'can do' attitude will reduce frustrations and tantrums.

Number, colour and shape recognition will be familiar to your child now and she will know the names of the common ones, identifying them when asked. Games that aid learning in this area are plentiful and your child will absorb far more through play than just being told the different colours. When you are out and about ask her to describe colours or shapes of everyday objects. Ask simple questions like: 'What colour is the postbox?' or 'What shape is that window?' If she hesitates for too long, limit her options, with: 'Is the postbox blue or red?' or 'Is the window square or circular?'

The ability to identify items by both shape and colour, such as a blue square, red circle or yellow triangle, is a sign that your child's cognitive skills are developing and she is able to process more complex information.

Books are beneficial and enjoyable for children of any age, and there is something wonderful about that special time just before bed when you cuddle up for a story. As well as all the benefits this routine has for emotional development, it also promotes cognitive skills. Encourage your child to think about and predict the next event in a new story book or think of an alternative ending for a familiar book. Her brain will be developed enough for her to understand what has just happened in a story and she will be able to build on this and predict what happens next. You can then enjoy reading the book together to see if she guessed correctly.

Using books with new vocabulary helps children develop their language and their thinking skills. There is an ongoing debate in the world of developmental psychology as to what comes first, thought or language. While this debate rages on, it is clear that there is a strong link between language and thought, each reinforcing the development of the other.

Your child will be beginning to understand, and show an awareness of, hazardous situations such as a hot cooker, cars driving along the street, falling off high structures and sharp knives or scissors. She may know the rules and try to abide by them in order to avoid getting hurt. For example, she will choose not to touch the cooker when it is on and will ask an adult for help while climbing on a wall. However, she will not know how to protect herself fully and may well be rather accident-prone so do make sure you take precautions to prevent serious injury. Teaching road safety is important around now as she will be walking along pavements rather than sitting in a buggy. She needs to learn never to run or step out into the road, so give her simple explanations to help her to understand the reasons for this vital rule.

## Social and emotional development

During this year it is common for your child to develop fears, especially at night. A child experiencing what are known as 'night terrors' may become very distressed while sleeping, often crying out loud, screaming and thrashing about, but have no recollection of the episode in the morning. Even though she may not remember the incident, try to chat with her about her dreams and make sure there is nothing worrying her subconsciously.

She may also develop fears that have previously not been present, maybe of dogs, creepy-crawlies or loud noises. Her imagination is really progressing now and, although this new thought process can be exciting, it can also be frightening and confusing – causing her to become unsettled and worried.

It is important to listen to how she is feeling. Try to understand what she is afraid of and why. Is she worried the dog may bite her or jump up at her? Has she witnessed a lively dog jump up at someone? The best thing you can do is reassure her and make her feel safe. We all know that daddy-long-legs won't hurt us but even as adults our fears are often irrational, and we all need to feel safe. Many fears are due to not knowing about or understanding something. Gently introduce her to the subject she is fearful of – perhaps read a book with dogs or creepy-crawlies in. Fact books are great at helping children gain knowledge and an awareness of subjects.

When your child seems more confident, try introducing whatever scares her again. Ask a friend who has a friendly dog if you can take it for a walk or just be in the same house as it. If you see a creepy-crawly, point it out to her and ask if she can identify what it is or count its legs. Hopefully the fear will eventually fade, but one main thing to remember is not to be too dramatic about it; don't provide too much attention when she is screaming with fear … gently pick her up and make her feel safe without pandering too much. Showing her you're not scared of the subject will be reassuring.

### Attachment

This age is a key time for emotional development, as your child will be securely attached, knowing where her home is or where she belongs. You will be aware that your child is developing well when she is able to feel secure in more than one environment and with more than one caregiver. Most children will have grown out of their clingy phase, but be prepared for periodic relapses when your child is ill, tired or anxious.

Children who are securely attached may show a willingness to explore and move increasing distances away from their caregiver but will frequently 'check in' with the main caregiver when in distress. On the other hand, children who lack secure attachment may seem very friendly and outgoing, as they will seek cuddles from anyone when they are distressed. This can seem an endearing trait in a child, but at this age it is more natural and desirable that she seeks comfort from one or two main caregivers.

### Development of identity

Social play promotes language and communication, and your three-year-old will love to play with her newly formed friendship groups, which will help her develop her identity as well as a sense of belonging and will boost her confidence.

Expressing herself through arts and crafts will also become appealing as her ability to draw and create more precise patterns and images develops.

### Personal hygiene and self-management

Personal hygiene is an important subject to teach your child, and now is the perfect time to start forming good, healthy routines. Your attitude to cleanliness will stay with her throughout life and will help avoid infections and medical complaints. A simple hygiene routine should be practised daily.

All of your child's baby teeth are likely to be through now, meaning more sleep (for everyone!) and fewer pain-related upsets. However, she now needs to learn to look after them and understand that dental hygiene is important for avoiding decay, fillings and cavities. Your child will not be able to understand the long-term effects as she lives very much in the here and now, but starting to introduce the concept of looking after your teeth so they last for your whole life is within her understanding. Avoid giving her sugary foods and drinks as much as possible, and ensure she brushes her teeth twice daily. Making brushing fun, by singing a song or making it into a game, will encourage your child to make it into a habit (something she does automatically) rather than a chore (something she will try to avoid doing if possible).

Bath time has so far been fun: toys and games have distracted her while you wash her body and hair, avoiding tears. However, she is now ready to start learning to do this independently. Help her to understand why we wash the mud off our knees and food from around our mouths and clean our feet. Smelling and feeling clean and fresh will help her to feel good about herself and is important for her self-esteem.

As your child gains confidence exploring the world, she will be touching more and more, picking up the bacteria and dirt that surround all of us. To avoid unnecessary infections or tummy bugs it is important that you teach her hygiene when it comes to washing her hands. Ensure she always washes her hands before and after eating or touching food – and essentially after any contact with animals (particularly farm animals). The use of soap and warm water will help remove dirt and germs.

Your child is now old enough to learn to blow her own nose when it is blocked but will need to be taught this. Blowing should be done in a gentle manner in order to avoid damage to sensitive blood vessels. If she struggles with the concept of blowing out through her nose rather than her mouth, ask her to pretend she is blowing out candles with her nose.

Make sure when she sneezes or coughs she knows to use a tissue if one is available – and if not to use the inside of her elbow, as this avoids spreading bacteria to other areas, particularly hands that touch other objects.

As mixing with other children is now more regular, she is more susceptible to catching head lice. Keep long hair tied back as much as possible, particularly when attending school and parties. The use of plenty of conditioner when washing her hair will also help to stop lice from staying in the hair. Regular use of a nit comb during bath time can help eliminate them, and ensure you highlight the problem to a teacher if she is infected. Discourage the sharing of hats or caps with peers.

## The power of a bear hug

With increasing reports of anti-social behaviour and children with mental-health issues, it is worth looking at toys that help children's emotional development.

Research going back over half a century shows the need young children have for comfort and emotional security. Emotional needs, such as comfort, love and attachment, are vital for children's development as, without them, children will not be able to develop their self-esteem, sense of identity and independence.

A loving environment with emotionally available caregivers and mutually rewarding relationships is the best thing a child can have, but there are other things that support a child's emotional development too.

Teddies are a popular first toy for babies, and the fact that they are so familiar to a child by the time she is old enough to have worries gives them huge amounts of emotional significance. Many adults remember particular teddies with affection because of their importance to their own childhood.

Smell is strongly linked to emotional memory and teddies that have been cuddled and slept with develop a very personal aroma, which children find comforting.

Teddies' soft feel makes them huggable and their faces give them a personality, unlike a comfort blanket, so children can transfer feelings to them. This can act as a substitute for a person when they have worries they want to work through. It's not that teddies can ever take the place of a caring adult, but late at night when the child is in bed and supposed to be going to sleep, cuddly toys can help a child relax and get a good night's sleep so that they are more able to get the most out of the following day.

Children are often afraid that their worries are silly and that adults won't understand. The very fact that pets and cuddly toys don't answer back makes them great listeners, and children are often able to work through their problems and find their own solutions simply by saying them out loud – this is the basis for most of the listening therapies (e.g. cognitive behavioural therapy) that are so popular today.

If parents spend time reading with their young child while the child cuddles a teddy bear, the child will associate the teddy with positive feelings of security, calmness, love and happiness, and so cuddling it can recreate those feelings and help a child cope with challenges they face, even when the parent is not there.

During periods of change or stress, parents should try not to wash the teddy too much and certainly not change the scent of the laundry detergent if the toy does need a wash. The smell of the teddy is all part of the comforting effect.

You can use soft toys to maintain continuity between a childcare setting and your child's home and enhance the settling-in process.

So, with all the high-tech toys available, spare a thought for a cuddly bear and help children develop into happy, emotionally healthy adults.

## Playful Activities

Now is a good time to start playing games with your child that involve sharing and turn-taking. Take your child through the steps, saying things like, 'Now it's my turn to build the tower, then it's your turn,' or, 'You share the red blocks with me, and I'll share the green blocks with you.'

## Memory game

This is brilliant at keeping children focused, improving concentration spans and developing memory skills. Place four or five objects in front of your child and ask her to remember what she can see. Give her 20 seconds or so to do this and then cover them over with a tea towel. Ask her to name all the objects that are under the cloth. If she can do this easily add more objects; if she struggles reduce the amount of objects she has to remember.

## Arts and crafts

Try to make creativity as varied and fun as possible by introducing various textures, colours and different materials. Glitter, clay, glue, materials and other adventurous textiles are excellent for creating different effects or shapes. The various textures encourage your child to use different muscles and skills to mould, sprinkle or paste her creations. Varying the consistencies will also teach her the notion of hard, soft, wet, dry, smooth and plenty more!

Encourage decision-making, asking your child what she wants to make and then getting her to choose the textiles she thinks would work best. For example, if she wants to make a dog, she may choose clay for the body and paint to colour it, or she may prefer to draw a dog and stick furry material to the paper to create a realistic feel.

Model-making with junk modelling items, such as toilet-roll tubes, empty yoghurt pots and old cereal packets, can offer endless entertainment while at the same time promoting fine motor skills, imagination and thinking skills.

## Chalk

As drawing is evolving, chalk can offer another fun activity. Chalk boards are useful to have but not essential as chalk can be used on patios or the garden walls. Give her a box of different colours and let her loose on your patio. It easily washes away with the rain so there's no mess for you to worry about either. This can be enjoyed with friends too, encouraging social engagement and language.

## The shopping game

This is a great memory game to play with your toddler. The first player says, 'I went to the shops and bought a dog [or whatever item they choose].' Then the second player has to repeat this but add on an extra item – perhaps: 'I went to the shop and bought a dog and a telephone.' The next players have to repeat all the previous items and add one of their own. Keep going until one player forgets an object.

## Word game

This is another fun game to play. The first person to start says any word they can think of. The other players then have to say another word related to the previous word. For example, the first word may be 'chocolate'; the next person could then say 'milk' and the following person may say 'drink' or 'white', and so on. If you're really good at this you can put a time limit on thinking (maybe 10 seconds).

## Role play and dressing up

Role-play props are brilliant at getting your child's imagination flowing, encouraging language development and helping her to develop a sense of self-identity. She can use dressing-up clothes or a doctor's kit to establish her knowledge of adult roles and her understanding of the world.

## It's show time!

Give your child a pretend microphone (a hairbrush or wooden spoon is good) and let her sing, tell a story or act, etc. You can be the audience and let her entertain you. This type of play is brilliant at boosting her confidence and self-esteem.

## Make-believe world

Children love a make-believe world and hunting for things they wish they could see. Woods are great for searching under the toadstools, in rotting parts of dead trees and by the roots of the old oak tree. Be imaginative with everything you come across … moss could be the fairies' beds, a hole in a tree could be their bath, etc. Embrace and feed your child's imagination.

## 'Pooh sticks'

When you are out with your toddler, try a game of 'Pooh sticks'. Find a low bridge that goes over a stream with a weak current. All players find an identifiable stick or leaf to play with. You then stand on the bridge and count to three. On three you all drop your stick or leaf into the water (the side where the water is running underneath the bridge), and then run to the other side of the bridge to see whose object comes out first and wins the race.

## Balancing act

Walking along garden walls, fallen trees and lines drawn in the park or playgrounds, will help your child practise her balancing abilities. On higher objects, such as walls, always be next to her in case she falls, and offer a hand when needed.

## Choosing Toys

### Tricycles or balance bikes

These are brilliant for this age group. The pedalling motion will strengthen gross motor skills, and steering will introduce them to directions, control and essential concentration (if they don't want to end up crashing!) All children learn to ride bikes at different ages (usually between three and eight) and this is mainly dependent on the amount of time they are given to practise. A child who spends regular weekends in the park with a bike is likely to learn quicker than a child who rarely practises.

Balance bikes are a great help in teaching children the balance required for pedal bikes.

### Jigsaw puzzles

These can be useful to teach turn-taking. Give two children a puzzle to complete and ask them to place one piece in each alternately. Eventually they will get used to the routine and learn that they can complete the full puzzle by working together.

### Outdoor toys

Instilling an outdoor and sporty approach can really help your child develop a healthy body and mental attitude. Hand–eye coordination can be honed in this field while hobbies and interests can start to flourish.

There are plenty of games that can be used to encourage outdoor play, such as footballs, lightweight tennis sets, achievable obstacle courses and a skipping rope.

## Farm toys

Farm toys are fantastic for both preschool girls and boys as they help children to learn through role play. Many children think that food just comes in wrappers and you get it from the shops; however, playing with farm toys will often produce questions and discussions about working on farms, animals, food production, etc., and can help children gain confidence by increasing their understanding of the world.

As preschool children vary greatly in their abilities and develop new skills very quickly, non-prescriptive toys such as farm toys enable them to play with the toys at their own level and in their own way. A younger child who is learning to speak can practise making the animal and machine noises, whereas an older, more able, child will be able to create imaginary scenarios and act them out cooperatively with peers. Farm toys also promote engagement and cooperation between the sexes. Giving free access to farm play to both boys and girls is the best way to let them choose their own play patterns.

## It Is Not Always Easy – Troubleshooting Tips

### 'My child won't share'

Most children are very egocentric and young children can seem quite selfish, but sharing is an important life skill. It is something children need to learn in order to make friends and play cooperatively.

Lots of children do not want to share their favourite toys, and one way of avoiding arguments is to help your child put their precious toys away when they have friends round and get out some things that are for everyone to play with. Make sure your child knows that she won't be asked to share her favourite toy but let her know you expect her to be kind and generous with her other toys.

Notice and praise good sharing in others too. You could say things like, 'Your friend was sharing her toys really well, and that was very kind of her.' Make sure your praise is genuine, immediate and focused. It's really powerful to say, 'Well done, you shared your building bricks really well. Did it feel nice to be helpful?' Teaching children to reflect on their own feelings from an early age will also develop self-awareness and empathy, both of which contribute to healthy social development.

Sharing and turn-taking are linked skills, and there are lots of activities that become accessible when your child can share. Let her join in with an activity, but if she won't share, stop the game and show her that you are sad about not being able to continue.

If children are fighting over a toy and not sharing, a reasonable consequence might be to remove the toy for a short period of time. They will learn that neither of them get what they want and eventually they will see the benefit in sharing. This approach also prevents any imbalance between siblings of different ages and promotes cooperation rather than rivalry or conflict between siblings.

By the age of three, many children will start to understand the concept of turn-taking but they might still get angry if another child takes a toy they want and find it a struggle to wait for their turn, so it's really important to notice and reinforce good behaviour here.

You can help your child to share by encouraging fairness. Children have a very black-and-white approach to justice – either it is right or it is wrong – and if they feel that the situation is fair they will be more likely to share.

Overall, it is important to be realistic about a young child's ability to share. At this age, most children are still very self-centred and have little understanding of other people's thoughts and emotions. Remember to give your child plenty of examples of good sharing, especially you sharing your things with her and explaining that you are doing so because 'that's what we do with friends and family'.

## 10 Fun Things to Do with Your Child

1. Feed a horse.
2. Pick your own strawberries and have them for pudding.
3. Take a rubber dinghy to a stream and let her have a float around.
4. Hunt for bugs and make a bug hotel.
5. Sleep in a tent.
6. Make her own 'George's marvellous medicine'.
7. Create a collage from things she finds in the garden.
8. Plant a seed and watch it grow.
9. Build a snowman.
10. Watch a film at the cinema.

## Making Memories

Has your child started to learn to ride a bike?

.......................................................................................................

What's your child's favourite outdoor activity?

.......................................................................................................

.......................................................................................................

.......................................................................................................

**play**

Who are your child's friends?

..................................................................................................

..................................................................................................

What is your child's favourite role-play game?

..................................................................................................

Does your child have problems sharing certain toys? Which ones?

..................................................................................................

..................................................................................................

## Your Notes

..................................................................................................

..................................................................................................

..................................................................................................

..................................................................................................

..................................................................................................

..................................................................................................

..................................................................................................

..................................................................................................

..................................................................................................

..................................................................................................

..................................................................................................

.......................................................................................

.......................................................................................

.......................................................................................

.......................................................................................

.......................................................................................

.......................................................................................

# Chapter Eight
# Starting School
# (4 Years and Onwards)

As children move towards their fifth birthday, school will become a big feature in their lives. Helping your child prepare for the start of school can have a massive impact on how well she settles in. Schools will often assess a child on entry to the school and use those tests as the basis for predicting progress and SAT results. While the school will adjust these predictions, it is beneficial for your child to start school confidently and settle in quickly in order to maximise her chances of academic success.

However, this is where many parents panic and make life unnecessarily difficult for themselves and their children. The key factors in settling well and getting school off to a good start are not what you may expect.

It doesn't matter if a child can read or write, or count to 100 in French! Teachers are well trained and fully expect to teach children these skills. What does make the difference is whether a child is able to follow instructions, concentrate, make friends, try new things and do things for herself, such as going to the toilet independently and putting on her own coat, shoes, etc. The good news is that all of these things are developed through play in the preceding years so parents can relax, resist the urge to 'hothouse' a child in preparation for school and enjoy playing and having fun together.

## What to Look Out for During this Stage

### Physical and sensory development

#### *Movement*
Control over muscles is getting more advanced so your child can now stand on one foot for a few seconds with reasonable balance. All movements seem to be more controlled and established, whether it be walking, running, jumping or climbing. She will be showing interest in new movements such as skipping, hopping on one foot and galloping, embracing all new skills introduced to her.

Try to get her to attempt forward rolls or swinging from bars (monkey bars and swings are great and often found in playgrounds).

Other skills she will be able to do on a basic level are using a scooter to get from A to B and pedalling a tricycle or bike with stabilisers. While the speed at which she travels will be dependent on strength and experience, she will become faster as she becomes more skilled.

As your child approaches her fifth birthday she will gain the confidence to try new, more adventurous movements, such as walking along beams or benches, using a skipping rope, roller skating and learning to ride a bike. Don't be afraid of the odd cut or bruise – all children have accidents throughout their childhood and it is important to remember that these are learning curves for your child.

Of course there are lots of activities that carry an element of risk and possible injury. Although it is vital that you minimise risks of serious injury, children can benefit in a really positive way if we let them learn for themselves and don't take the element of fun, adventure and daring out of everything because we are afraid of them hurting themselves!

### Coordination

Fine motor skills are continuing to develop, and continuous encouragement to strengthen these is still beneficial. Drawing and painting are still as popular as ever with this age group and should be developed and engaged in as much as possible, along with more complex model-making using old household objects. Not only will this engage your child's imagination but it will further improve her concentration and muscle movements.

'Pincer grip' activities will strengthen the essential muscles needed for writing, and activities such as using child-safe scissors or threading beads on to a string can help in this area. As your child approaches school age, it is important to embrace as many skills as possible that will help her settle into school life. Play involving Play-Doh, gluing and painting will all help strengthen the muscles in her hands and promote further finger control.

### Food and drink

As she approaches school age your child's brain will be working hard, absorbing information and learning every day. In order to maximise her learning capacity you need to provide her with all the different food groups, with the emphasis being on those with particular nutritional value, such as fresh fruit, vegetables, dairy, pulses, lean meats, fish, and wholegrain cereals and bread.

Junk food should be eliminated. Although ready meals may seem quick, cheap and easy to cook, the nutritional value is low so such meals should be kept to an absolute minimum. There are plenty of recipes that are just as quick and easy to cook and that are far more nutritious, and instilling a healthy food attitude in your child could be classed as one of the most important things you do for her. With obesity being a major problem in young children, it is even more important to set an example of healthy eating to your child.

It may start to become more difficult to keep sugary foods and drinks at bay as your child becomes more aware of their availability via their widening social circle. There are several options of healthy snacks that are widely available these days to help parents with this problem. Dried fruit can be purchased in funky packets and differing shapes to help children recognise these as treats. Flavoured rice cakes are an excellent alternative to crisps.

Family mealtimes are really valuable – they are an ideal time of day to communicate together and have quality family time. However, they are quite often overlooked due to busy lives. Working parents should try to utilise weekends for this as much as possible and ensure that childcare settings include family-style mealtimes.

Now is a perfect time to encourage good table manners by setting good examples. Your child should be able to hold her cutlery correctly, using each piece appropriately. You will find that by enforcing basic manners they will become second nature as she grows: for example, not talking with a full mouth, using a napkin to wipe mouths (not hands or sleeves!), elbows off the table, and feet and legs under the table.

## Thinking and communication

### Thinking

Your child will now be able to comprehend more complex concepts, such as highest, lowest, largest, widest and longest as well as opposites. She will be able to point to the correct answer when asked, 'Which one is the largest elephant?' and will provide the correct answer when asked, 'What is the opposite of big?'

She will be able to think of words that rhyme with each other – for example when asked, 'What rhymes with cat?' she could suggest rat, bat or sat. She will like rhymes and coming up with new rhyming words. She may even enjoy making up nonsense words that rhyme with your word such as 'gat' or 'dat'.

Many children of this age will be able to identify certain letters, particularly those in their name, and will be able to recognise them in different words and when written down. Their ABC skills will be honed once they are at school. Some children may now be able to put their knowledge of recognising letters together and show signs of starting to read basic books with a few three-letter words on each page.

Children will be learning to count, and will possibly be counting up to 10 or even beyond correctly, and may even recognise the numbers when written down. Try to look for numbers when you are out and about and ask your child what they are – for example, door numbers, car registration plates or prices on items in the shops.

Do not worry if your child isn't yet interested in learning to read or count; she will be given plenty of help with this at school and the last thing you want to do is put her off learning these skills by pushing her before she is ready.

Children often find starting school extremely tiring. Your child's brain will be absorbing a lot of new information, rules and behavioural expectations, as well as coping with a new environment and social experience. Alongside this her body is still growing fast, which is also tiring and demands plenty of rest. Although it is very tempting to put a tired child in the front of the TV for some 'quiet time', there are plenty of other measures you can use to give your child the rest her body needs. Sleep is a key factor here and plays a large part in behaviour, learning and development. It is much healthier for a child to be active all day and go to bed early than flop on the sofa after school and stay there for hours. Try to limit TV time and encourage other 'quiet activities', such as reading together, colouring or doing a puzzle.

### Language

Speech will be really coming along now and your child may have a vocabulary of over 1,000 words. Sentences will be becoming more complex too – for example, your child will be able to communicate what she has done today and who she played with, as well as starting to show an understanding of the past, present and future tenses. She will also be able to define the difference. For example, 'I'm going to play in the garden', 'I played with Sam at school today'. She will also be able to use descriptive words to express basic feelings, such as 'happy' or 'sad'.

Repeating a whole nursery rhyme from memory is now possible too and children of this age will enjoy singing the songs they have learnt with you.

It is important not just to develop your child's verbal communication skills but also to focus on listening, understanding and writing skills, as well as her ability to respond to questions.

Role play and drama will be a key feature in children's play at this stage, and such play is wonderful at enhancing their communication skills, helping them to express their ideas and opinions and work collaboratively with others. While role playing, your child will tend to make shows and routines up as she goes along, rather than plan a show, as her cognitive skills are not yet developed enough. You could introduce props such as clothing, umbrellas or bags to add more substance for her.

Role play can also be a tool to ease anxiety and prepare children for the next stage. For example, playing 'schools', being teacher and taking the register can help establish routines and concepts she may be about to face.

## Social and emotional development

Social development is one of the most important areas of development for preschool children, and traditionally it's been undervalued in favour of hothousing school-based subjects such as numeracy and literacy. Toys and games that encourage social interaction such as sharing, turn-taking and communication are really great for this age group.

Your child will be gathering confidence in her social awareness and start to recognise certain friendships rather than just play with the person standing next to her. She may choose activities to participate in because her friends are doing it rather than because she wants to do it. By starting to form opinions on peers, she is also establishing who she likes and gets on with and those that she doesn't bond as well with.

As she starts school, she will develop a strong desire to 'fit in' and be liked by her peers. She will be discovering her own identity, maybe copying traits of her peers while exploring new ways of doing things, all of which are influenced by her social environment. Trying different clubs and participating in after-school activities can help form hobbies and interests and will help shape her own identity.

Having a 'best' friend is popular now and she will love to chat about what she and her 'best friend' have done. Don't be shocked though when the 'best friend' changes regularly.

This new interaction with others will introduce children to the different opinions, rules and methods of play of their peers. However, they may struggle with understanding the different ways and not be overly willing to adapt or adjust their own methods just yet.

Separation anxiety and seemingly irrational fears are common around this age as children start school and find their feet in a much wider community. During any period of change it can be helpful to maintain as much consistency as possible. Don't be surprised if a child seems to regress and seeks comfort from familiar toys that she appeared to have grown out of previously.

### *Development of identity*

By now your child will have a strong sense of who she is, who her friends are, what she enjoys doing and what she looks like. She will be able to identify certain features of herself to you or others when asked. For example, she will identify her age, eye colour and hair colour. She may also be able to make certain comparisons between herself and her friends – e.g. 'I am taller than Ella but shorter than Miko' or 'Katie has blonde hair but mine is brown'. Asking her to look in the mirror and draw a self-portrait can be an excellent way of encouraging her to look at her features and make further observations.

She will know about certain cultures (particularly her own or her friends') and know how they can differ. Try to talk to her about how people can be different, how different cultures may wear unusual clothes, may look different to you and may eat different foods.

She may be starting to recognise or stare at people in the street who look different to her – maybe they are in a wheelchair or have a distractive physical feature. It is natural for your child to stare and, although this may make you feel awkward, it is important to allow her to look. Explain in simple language how this person differs to her and why this may be. Avoid statements such as 'don't stare' or 'keep walking'. Children shouldn't learn to avoid eye contact or be afraid to ask questions; this is all a learning curve for them. When discussing differences in people, be sensitive but also matter of fact.

Your child should by now know the difference between 'right' and 'wrong' or 'good' and 'bad', and she will have certain ideologies that place different people into the different subheadings. For example, burglars are 'bad' people and the police are 'good' people. She will hopefully identify herself as 'good'; however, she will struggle with the concept that some people can be both 'good' and 'bad'. Morality is very black and white at this stage – it is not until children get towards the end of primary school that they can see that there are degrees of morality and that people or actions are rarely wholly good or bad.

Emotional development is incredibly important around this age and every confidence boost you can provide her with will have a really positive impact on her ongoing self-esteem and confidence. As she tries to fit in among her peer group it is also valuable to ensure she is confident enough to be herself and not just copy how her friends behave, dress or what they do for interests.

Playing with both genders has been the norm until now, but as she reaches the ages of four and five she will start to recognise more differences between girls' and boys' play and will move towards solely playing with her own gender. She will predominantly play with this gender until she is around 12.

Introducing hobbies and interests can be beneficial. She will now be able to express certain interests and likes towards specific items or activities, and it is important to encourage these for her self-identification and development. Be prepared for hobbies and crazes to change frequently.

## Playful Activities

### Role play

Try using your child's interest in role play to help ease any anxieties or stress that she may be experiencing. Between four and five is a common time for anxiety to surface relating to a new environment she will be entering (i.e. school), as well as sadness for leaving the nursery or the preschool she has grown so familiar with. By using a 'schools' role play you will help her adapt to her new routines more easily. For example, she could play at being the teacher and you could be the pupil. (Ensure you make it as fun and exciting as possible so she can start looking forward to all the positives school can bring.)

Whether your child engages in a make-believe world of princesses, fairies, superheroes or pirates, or enjoys playing with action figures, try to embrace it as much as possible and find as many props or old clothes around the home as you can to enable the role play to become even more real for her. Promoting her interest in drama and the arts can really help with her confidence, imagination, self-identification and understanding of the world.

### Collections

Collecting items is a great way for children to learn many essential life skills. Whatever your child chooses to collect – be it shells, stones or shop-bought figures – she will find several ways of organising them, she will count them regularly (if not several times a day), interact with other children who collect things and, if it is one of the many shop-bought crazes such as branded trading cards/figures, she will be encouraged through peers to negotiate and swap any doubles she owns.

## Arts and crafts

As your child's capabilities with arts and crafts improve try to look for more intricate activities for her to participate in as she will want to achieve a quality end product but may still need some help.

Glitter art or sand art can offer her an exciting new task – although it's simple to do, the pictures look great and she will be really proud of her creations. Mosaics can also offer an excellent final piece but are simple enough for a child over the age of four to create (these can also help with number recognition and thinking skills).

Painting is still a popular, fun pastime, although, at this stage, children can try more than just painting on plain paper. Encourage your child to decorate a shoe box that can be used for storing her pens, a plant pot for the garden or make some plaster of Paris models for her room. She will love being able to use her creations for useful purposes.

## Mirror games and self-identification

Although children are more aware of themselves and who they are at this age, their knowledge is still limited and can sometimes just include what they see directly. For example, when you play hide and seek, you will often find a four-year-old will hide her head and face but leave her legs in full view – if she can't see you she assumes you can't see her! Or she may tell you where she is about to hide.

Using a full-length mirror, ask your child to take a good look at her reflection, question her on what she can see and then get her to draw a picture of herself, including her legs, arms and head. This activity will focus her attention on the different parts of the body and make her more aware of her own body.

Play dressing-up games and pay particular attention to the whole body rather than just her face and head.

### 'Simon says'

Following instructions, listening to commands and paying attention are all skills expected at school. Your four-year-old should be able to do all of these, although she will sometimes choose not to, and she may need a bit of practice.

'Simon says' offers your child a really fun game, which requires all these skills in order for her to win the game. In order to play, you need a 'leader' who will stand in front of the other players and give them instructions to follow. The leader gives instructions in two ways, either: 'Simon says, "Touch your toes"' or 'Touch your toes' (missing out 'Simon says'). The group of children following the instructions should *only* carry out the command if the leader has said 'Simon says' first. If you get it wrong you are out. You keep going until you only have one person left – they are the winner!

If you mix the game up a bit you can develop your child's motor and coordination skills at the same time. Try 'Simon says, "Stand on one leg"' or 'Simon says, "Hop up and down"'. Be as inventive as possible.

## 'Name it'

Choose a category such as 'food'. Take turns to name all the foods you can think of in 15 seconds. For example, you say, 'Banana,' then she says, 'Pasta.' Keep going until one of you can't think of anything else within the 15 seconds (that person loses). This is great for developing thinking skills and verbal fluency.

## 'Guess the tune'

Another fun game to play is to hum a well-known nursery rhyme or song, such as 'Twinkle Twinkle, Little Star' or 'Humpty Dumpty', and get your child to guess the song. This promotes listening skills as well as musical development.

## Gardening

Your child may now be starting to show an interest in plants and the garden. Offer her a little patch of the garden just for her, take her to the garden centre to choose some plants and let her dig the holes and plant them. Ensure she looks after them correctly by watering them frequently (but not too much). Food plants such as tomatoes, peas or beans are easy to grow and great to eat once they are ready. It will show her where we get food from and can also help with children who don't want to eat their veggies! If you don't have access to a garden, use pots on windowsills – cress is simple to grow in small pots and perfect for a kitchen sill.

## Home-made volcano

On a tray make a volcano shape using modelling clay. The clay needs to be hollowed out most of the way down but a hole about the size of a large coin needs to be kept at the top. Press the modelling clay firmly on to the tray at the bottom to prevent any leakages. Put 1 teaspoon of bicarbonate of soda inside the hollowed-out volcano. Mix 1 teaspoon of red food colouring and 3 teaspoons of vinegar together in a jug. Here comes the explosion – carefully pour the food colouring and vinegar solution into the volcano and see what happens.

Your child will really enjoy this simple science experiment; explain that the carbon dioxide gas given off by the mixture of bicarbonate of soda and vinegar causes the eruption.

## Making 'gloop'

Pour some cornflour into a large bowl or tray. Mix in some water (a little at a time) until it has turned into a thick paste. This will now be hard if you squeeze it and a liquid if you let it trickle through your fingers. It's a very weird texture that you have to experience to understand. You can add food colouring or glitter if you want to make it more interesting.

## Cooking

Cooking can be really useful at providing your child with a further interest in food (particularly if she is a fussy eater). Ask her to help you with preparing foods for dinner, possible chopping, peeling and/or breaking eggs. Aprons will help avoid messy clothes, and specially designed children's cooking utensils can make mixing and baking easier for her to manage alone.

You can also get your child to make cakes, biscuits and flapjacks that are simple enough for her to do predominantly by herself (with you watching of course). All of this is great for developing numeracy and literacy skills as children learn to read recipes, measure and weigh quantities.

**Picnic adventure**

Go for a picnic in the park; however, get her to take charge and create the picnic. Take her shopping and ask her to decide what to put in the picnic (although make sure there is a balance of healthy options too). She can make the sandwiches, prepare the fruit and pack the picnic hamper. If you are feeling very adventurous, let her make invitations and ask some friends along.

**Swings**

Swings can offer so many benefits for your child. Her gross motor skills and hand grip will be strengthened. She will learn how to coordinate her legs in time to get the swing to go higher – promoting body control and experiencing 'cause and effect'.

Sharing is a great lesson to teach using a swing – children can take turns to push one another and communicate if they want to go faster or slower.

## Construction play

Have you ever felt satisfied when you finished building something? Well, so do children. Construction play is an organised type of play that is goal-orientated. It provides high levels of satisfaction and achievement, which increases children's confidence and provides a sense of success, meaning that they will want to repeat the exercise.

Children learn through trial and error, and construction play enables the manipulation of objects to suit their needs and make materials become purposeful. Construction play can be simple at a toddler level just by stacking blocks, but construction creations increase in complexity with age and ability, creating 3D spaceships and models out of Lego.

Construction play encourages children to stack, mould, connect, rearrange, assemble and disassemble, and teaches children the importance of spatial concepts. Through this understanding their mathematical language develops and they learn to use terms such as below, on top, beside and above. Children also learn to distinguish between shapes, sizes, colours and the usefulness of something.

Cooperative construction play promotes socially savvy children as they support other players by recognising each other's strengths and weaknesses. Children often develop roles within the group and the 'leader' will delegate roles to another according to their ability, thus developing leadership skills.

Regular engagement with construction toys develops children's divergent thinking skills (their problem-solving, logic and creativity skills) without adult intervention. These skills are valuable in all aspects of their life, particularly as they get older.

What can parents do to support and extend their child's construction play experiences?

1.  Get involved: parents can play in unity with their child, by modelling different types of construction, thus giving children ideas.
2.  Provide a variety of materials that children can use to extend their construction such as building blocks, Lego, empty boxes or clean yoghurt pots. This develops creativity through being inquisitive

and experimental and allows children to think about different qualities of the resources and how these could be manipulated.

3.  Set a task or give your child an idea, but do not dictate by saying things like, 'Why don't you build a car garage to store your cars in?' This task could be carried out as a team, which will promote cooperative play and enhance social skills, as there is a shared goal. A team approach will also decrease individual competitiveness.

4.  Children learn through trial and error so leave your child to investigate and explore for herself.

5.  Ask questions to promote discussion so your child thinks about her choices: 'That looks great! What made you choose to use the colour red for your barn roof?'

6.  Encourage your child to visualise her creation and plan ahead.

7.  Provide play spaces that are safe and accessible to her.

8.  Encourage your child to tidy up after herself.

## Choosing Toys

### Small-world or play sets

Small-world sets, such as dolls' houses, car garages and farmyard sets, can be used to help encourage your child to understand the world. She will use the toys to recreate situations and experiences she has already encountered using her imagination and creative abilities. Now that her language has developed, you may hear her using different voices for different characters, noises for the animals or transport, and she may even copy sentences that she has learnt from you or her teacher to create a story.

Problem-solving is one of the great benefits of playing with small-world toys, as children learn how to overcome situations they are faced with, such as two cars not fitting down a ramp together. She will also learn 'cause and effect', realising that if she puts a figure on a slide it will slide down. She will be able to predict certain cause-and-effect motions while learning new ones.

Small-world toys are great at creating independent play. Children are far more likely to go off alone and play with these types of toys than any others. They don't need friends to play with these and often require little adult direction. Keeping the variety of these toys vast creates knowledge and understanding of all the different worlds.

## Pedal bikes (with stabilisers)

At around the age of four, children will be starting to show enough coordination and strength to ride a pedal bike with stabilisers, and many parents will jump at the chance to get them started.

We can all remember our first bike and the hours spent in the park with our parents or carers practising (and the sobs and bruises that inevitably followed!) Learning how to ride a bike has become a childhood milestone and a very important one. Not only does cycling promote independence and activity in children, it also teaches balance, posture control, coordination and development of motor skills. The skills required to cycle can be learnt at any age and expanded on as the child gets older and more competent.

There are plenty of products on the market that can help promote the essentials required, including:

- **Ride-ons**: These toys are not only fun, they will also help to encourage concentration, improve mobility, build confidence and promote exercise at a young age.
- **Scooters**: these are a great craze that promote balance and coordination (plus they will make a slow journey to school far quicker!) As your child gets better, the two-wheeled scooter can be introduced, building on her balance techniques and introducing more advanced steering systems.
- **Balance bikes**: these are great as a first bike as children can concentrate on balancing while learning to steer without the added complication of pedalling. Moving on to a larger bike will seem far less daunting after this.

## Jigsaw puzzles

There are so many jigsaw puzzles on the market that it is important to choose one that challenges your child but isn't so hard that she can't finish it without a lot of adult assistance. Most puzzles are labelled with an appropriate age but you will know whether your child could easily do an age 5+ puzzle or needs an easier one. Puzzles not only hone your child's fine motor skills but they also help with concentration and cognitive development.

If sharing is still proving an issue for your child, try getting her to do a puzzle with you or a friend. Taking turns at this stage could show her the positive outcome that can be achieved from teamwork and this key skill will help her settle even more easily into school.

## Construction sets

Models and creations will be getting more advanced now and children of this age may be able to follow simple instructions to create a particular box set, especially when using picture clues.

Construction toys still offer the benefits of pincer-grip development, creative imagination and fine motor skills. Keep the amount varied though so your child doesn't lose attention or interest and check sets are age-appropriate so she doesn't become too overwhelmed and gain a fear of failing. Lego, K'NEX, Meccano – to name just a few! – all offer different techniques of construction but each develop a child's skills just as well. For more on the benefits of construction play, see page 180.

## Board games

These continue to be a firm family favourite. Endless fun can be had playing the same games over and over again, and the quality family time gained from this is valuable to everyone. As well as communication and bonding being improved, the concept of friendly and gentle competition is introduced to your child (which she will need to learn to cope with when she starts school and also later in life!) Once again, ensure you choose a board game that is age-appropriate. A child's confidence can be damaged if you provide her with games she finds really tricky and she will get bored very quickly if it is too easy.

Find a game that offers educational benefits too – perhaps one that requires number or letter recognition, counting or adding (one with a dice can offer all of these).

## Imaginative toys

Dolls' houses, dumper trucks, doctor's kits, kitchens, toolboxes, puppets and action figures all represent an imaginative world to your child, and she will have endless fun recreating a world away from reality by incorporating these toys.

Role play can be made more interesting and creative by introducing different props, clothes and characters that will prompt new ideas – transporting her even deeper into the world of imagination and make-believe!

A lot of role-play toys feature everyday models such as a post-office play set, pop-up school or shop, etc., and it is lovely (and often very funny) to watch children participate and act out the ideologies they have subconsciously adopted.

Imagination is a truly powerful skill to have and can help your child in so many different ways. By continuing (or starting) drama or an interest in the arts, her thought process and language is engaged, and well-rounded communication and social skills can be learnt.

## Interactive toys

The benefits of interactive toys for your child are numerous. She will love being able to make things move, sing, fly or light up just by pressing a button.

From a walking dog on an electronic lead, dolls that talk, cry and soil their nappy to remote-controlled helicopters, the choice is endless and the ones you choose are solely dependent on your child and her interests.

## Toys to help develop numeracy

Numeracy will be a big topic for your child when she starts school. Offering her a head start in this area can really boost her confidence and help overcome the anxieties that she may already be feeling.

There are so many games and toys that can assist with teaching recognition of numbers, adding and subtracting and counting – it is all about finding one that she enjoys playing. Try using a variety of resources to aid your teaching and for her to start recognising that numbers are all around us. For example, number puzzles, clocks, toy telephones or fabric calendars.

Particularly beneficial games are those that require counting objects, using money or even telling the time. These will all help her to understand the basic, everyday mathematical ideas and skills required.

## Toys to help literacy skills

Literacy covers a large range of skills, from language development, spelling and reading through to writing. Choose games or toys that reinforce the areas your child needs help with – whether it is letter games that promote spelling or word games that encourage reading. Magnetic letters that can be stuck to your fridge can help with spelling her name or you can make funny sentences with them.

Games where she matches words with pictures can either be bought or home-made. If you want to make your own, find a few items around the house and put them on a table. On separate cards write the names of these items and ask her to match them to the correct item. Choose easy words to start with, such as 'pen', 'book', 'cup' or 'plate' and, as her ability increases, you can make them harder.

## It Is Not Always Easy – Troubleshooting Tips

### 'My child is anxious about starting school'

Starting school will be daunting for even the most confident and outgoing child. Therefore it is even more important for you to settle those fears and help your child become excited and keen to enter this new phase.

If you think she is suffering with nerves, try to find a couple of children going to the same school and organise a few play dates in the summer holidays. Seeing a few friendly faces on her first day will really help her feel more secure and safe.

As we mentioned before, role play can be a brilliant tool at exposing a child to new routines and life events in a light-hearted manner. Try role reversal while playing 'school' – where your child becomes the teacher and you are the pupil – to help the child understand her new environment and world.

Let her help you buy her uniform and new school shoes – i.e. choosing the dress or shirts she likes the most. Read her books about starting school; there are plenty of topical books on the market that target prominent milestones in a child's life and starting school is one of them. Choose a selection of books that you think she will enjoy and read them together. Talking to your child is the best way to settle any fears she may have about starting school. Bedtime is a lovely time of day to chat with your child and you will find she will talk far more openly at this time than any other. Both of you are relaxed, there are fewer distractions and hopefully the house is far quieter than during the day. Lie next to her on bed and ask her about all the things she is looking forward to at school (ensure you discuss only positives for a while). Finally ask her what she is not looking forward to – if there is anything that she is finding scary or changes that are worrying her, etc.

No matter how you think your child is going to cope with starting school, the most valuable thing you can do for her is to help her to feel safe, secure and excited about entering this new chapter. Reassure her that she is going to have plenty of fun, make lovely new friends and learn lots of new things.

## 'My child can't ride a bike but lots of her friends can'

All children will learn the skills needed to ride a bike at different stages so it is important to try not to compare her with others. Riding a bike requires a lot of confidence too, so maybe try to boost this at every available opportunity.

Try to find a fun, new place to practise: a park with a grassy slope, on holiday or a play area where they allow bikes. Keep the stabilisers on for a while and get her used to the new terrain and environment. Once you feel she is ready to try without help you can take them off.

Use an exciting destination for her to cycle to: maybe a favourite toy or a tree she can climb if she makes it.

Ask other parents with children who are also learning to ride a bike to join you. A bit of healthy competition may be just what she needs to spur her on.

Take an older sibling or friend who can already ride a bike with you. They can show her how much fun you can have once this skill is accomplished and she will also see that cycling is safe.

## 10 Fun Things to Do with Your Child

1. Collect leaves and make prints with them with paint.
2. Let her climb a tree.

3. Fly a kite.
4. Make a daisy chain.
5. Grow some vegetables and eat them for tea.
6. Go fossil hunting.
7. Take her for a pony ride.
8. Go outdoor ice skating at Christmas time.
9. Let her run under a sprinkler in the garden.
10. See a show at the theatre.

## Making Memories

What is your child most looking forward to about starting school?

..................................................................................................

..................................................................................................

What are her fears and anxieties about starting school?

..................................................................................................

..................................................................................................

How are you feeling about her starting school? (E.g. sad, excited, lonely?)

..................................................................................................

..................................................................................................

What vegetables has she grown herself and eaten?

..................................................................................................

..................................................................................................

How many letters and numbers can she recognise?

........................................................................................

........................................................................................

## Your Notes

........................................................................................

........................................................................................

........................................................................................

........................................................................................

........................................................................................

........................................................................................

........................................................................................

........................................................................................

........................................................................................

........................................................................................

........................................................................................

........................................................................................

........................................................................................

........................................................................................

........................................................................................

........................................................................................

........................................................................................

........................................................................................

# Final words

Ensuring your family life is fun and exciting not only makes your time together more enjoyable it also helps your child develop her key skills.

Children's learning is optimised when they are relaxed and feel secure. Play promotes both of these emotional states, and therefore allows your child to reach her full potential in a relaxed, fun and safe environment.

No one is saying parenting is a laugh a minute but hopefully the ideas in this book will help address and support you with some of the inevitable issues and stressful times that you will face throughout your journey as a parent.

Bringing fun into family life extends to adults as well as the children. It is important that you take time to identify all the things you enjoy doing and ensure you incorporate these activities into your schedule for your children to enjoy too. You will be benefitting your child by providing her with a model of emotional health and stability, giving her a blueprint to make herself happy.

In addition, activities and behaviours that feel good are more likely to be repeated – so the fun, and the associated developmental benefits, will become self-perpetuating.

Providing your child with a healthy, balanced play diet (see page 141) will be one way in which you can help give your child the best start in life as she embarks on her school career with a wide range of skills, enabling her to take advantage of all that school has to offer and providing a solid foundation upon which she will build further skills.

No matter how you choose to use this book, and which advice and play ideas you decide to adopt, remember that all children develop at different rates. Try to resist the temptation to compare your child to siblings or friends and try to boost her confidence and sense of self-worth at every opportunity.

If you do have any serious concerns about your child's development, please seek medical advice as soon as possible. Although, thankfully, many concerns are often unfounded, if your child is suffering from developmental delays it is best to get help as early as possible.

The most important thing is to enjoy your child ... she will be an adult before you know it. Allowing her to enjoy her childhood will help her become the adult you want her to be.

# Endnotes

1 Hughes, John et al, 'The "Mozart effect" on Epileptiform Activity', *Perceptual and Motor Skills*, vol. 86 (1998), p 835

2 Carmona, Richard H., Surgeon General, 'The Growing Epidemic of Childhood Obesity', testimony before the Subcommittee on Competition, Infrastructure, and Foreign Commerce and the Committee on Commerce, Science, and Transportation at the United States Senate (2 March 2004), as cited in www.surgeongeneral.gov/news/testimony/childobesity03022004.html

3 NSPCC, 'Listening to Children: Improving communication with your child', leaflet produced in 2013

4 Alexander, Gerianne and Hines, Melissa, 'Sex differences in response to children's toys in nonhuman primates (*Cercopithecus aethiops sabaeus*)', *Evolution and Human Behavior*, vol. 23, issue 6 (2002), pp 467–479, http://dx.doi.org/10.1016/S1090-5138(02)00107-1

# Appendix
# Nursery Rhymes
# and Verses

### 'Round and Round the Garden'

Round and round the garden,
Like a teddy bear.
*(Actions: using your forefinger, draw a circle on your child's palm and keep going around while you sing)*
One step, two step,
Tickle you under there!
*(Using your forefinger and middle finger, step slowly up to the top of their arm and give them a little tickle underneath)*

### 'This Little Piggy'

This little piggy went to market, *(Wiggle the 'big' toe)*
This little piggy stayed at home, *(Wiggle the 'second' toe)*
This little piggy had roast beef, *(Wiggle the 'middle' toe)*
This little piggy had none, *(Wiggle the 'fourth' toe)*
And this little piggy cried 'wee wee wee' all the way home.
*(Wiggle the 'little' toe and tickle the leg up to her tummy)*

## 'Oranges and Lemons'

'Oranges and lemons,'
Say the bells of St Clement's.
'You owe me five farthings,'
Say the bells of St Martin's.
'When will you pay me?'
Say the bells of Old Bailey.
'When I grow rich,'
Say the bells of Shoreditch.
'When will that be?'
Say the bells of Stepney.
'I do not know,'
Says the great bell of Bow.
Here comes a candle to light you to bed,
And here comes a chopper to chop off your head!

## 'Head, Shoulders, Knees and Toes'

*(Actions: point using both hands to each of the body parts when sung)*
Head, shoulders, knees and toes,
Knees and toes.
Head, shoulders, knees and toes,
Knees and toes,
And eyes and ears and mouth and nose.
Head, shoulders, knees and toes,
Knees and toes.

### 'Little Miss Muffet'

Little Miss Muffet
Sat on a tuffet,
Eating her curds and whey;
Along came a spider,
Who sat down beside her
And frightened Miss Muffet away.

### 'The Wheels on the Bus'

*(Actions: Move your arms round like you would a train)*
The wheels on the bus go round and round,
Round and round, round and round.
The wheels on the bus go round and round,
All day long.
*(Actions: Sway your arms in front of you like wipers)*
The wipers on the bus go swish, swish, swish.
Swish swish swish, swish swish swish.
The wipers on the bus go swish, swish, swish,
All day long.
*(Actions: Place your hands together like a prayer. Open your hands on 'open' and close them again on 'shut' – like a door)*
The door on the bus goes open and shut,
Open and shut, open and shut.
The door on the bus goes open and shut,
All day long.
*(Actions: Gently push your nose on 'Beep')*
The horn on the bus goes beep beep beep,
Beep beep beep, beep beep beep.
The horn on the bus goes beep beep beep,
All day long.

*(Actions: Stand up and sit down)*
The people on the bus go up and down,
Up and down, up and down.
The people on the bus go up and down,
All day long.
*(Actions: Rub your eyes pretending to cry)*
The babies on the bus go 'wah wah wah',
'Wah wah wah', 'wah wah wah'.
The babies on the bus go 'wah wah wah',
All day long.
*(Actions: Put your forefinger to your lips)*
The Daddies on the bus go 'shhh shhh shhh',
'Shhh shhh shhh', 'shhh shhh shhh'.
The daddies on the bus go, 'shhh shhh shhh',
All day long.

## 'Old MacDonald Had a Farm'

Old MacDonald had a farm, E-I-E-I-O,
And on that farm he had a cow, E-I-E-I-O,
With a 'moo moo' here and a 'moo moo' there.
Here a 'moo', there a 'moo', everywhere a 'moo moo'.
Old MacDonald had a farm, E-I-E-I-O.
Old MacDonald had a farm, E-I-E-I-O,
And on that farm he had a dog, E-I-E-I-O,
With a 'woof woof' here and a 'woof woof' there.
Here a 'woof', there a 'woof', everywhere a 'woof woof'.
Old MacDonald had a farm, E-I-E-I-O.
Old MacDonald had a farm, E-I-E-I-O,
And on that farm he had a cat, E-I-E-I-O,
With a 'meow meow' here and a 'meow meow' there.
Here a 'meow', there a 'meow', everywhere a 'meow meow'.

Old MacDonald had a farm, E-I-E-I-O.
Old MacDonald had a farm, E-I-E-I-O,
And on that farm he had a sheep, E-I-E-I-O,
With a 'baa baa' here and a 'baa baa' there.
Here a 'baa', there a 'baa', everywhere a 'baa baa'.
Old MacDonald had a farm, E-I-E-I-O.
*You can continue this song with any animals you like.*

### 'Humpty Dumpty'

Humpty Dumpty sat on a wall,
Humpty Dumpty had a great fall,
All the king's horses and all the king's men,
Couldn't put Humpty together again.

### 'This is the Way the … Ride'

This is the way the ladies ride,
Clip clop, clip clop.
*(Bounce your child gently and slowly on your knee)*
This is the way the gentlemen ride,
Trit trot, trit trot.
*(Bounce her faster)*
This is the way the farmers ride,
Hobbledee, hobbledee …
*(Really bounce her)*
And down in the ditch!
*(Drop your child slightly through your knees, but make sure she doesn't fall)*
*There are many variations to this rhyme, but this is a basic example – you can use whatever sound effects you like for the different riders!*

# Resources

I have put together the following list of resources, which I believe may be useful to you for further advice, information, local services and general support for parents.

## General child and family information

### BabyCentre
An online resource for new and expectant parents, providing a wealth of information on a wide range of topics, from conception to preschool.
www.babycentre.co.uk

### BBC Learning
Advice on how to support your child's education.
www.bbc.co.uk/schools/parents

### Bookstart
A literacy programme providing free book packs and parental guidance to help your baby enjoy reading.
www.bookstart.org.uk

### British Toy and Hobby Association and Toy Fair
Information on the safety standards for toys.
www.btha.co.uk

### CBeebies website
A collection of games, songs and clips for preschoolers.
www.bbc.co.uk/cbeebies

### Foundation Years
Information and support for parents through pregnancy to children aged five.
www.foundationyears.org.uk/parents

### Fundamentally Children
Advice and resources for helping children develop skills through play. Home of the Good Toy Guide and Good App Guide
www.fundamentallychildren.com

### Guardian Lifestyle: Family
Articles on family lifestyle issues.
www.theguardian.com/lifeandstyle/family

### Home-Start
A family support charity providing support and advice through a number of local centres.
www.home-start.org.uk

### Local Library services
Many local libraries hold baby and toddler sessions, as well as providing a range of baby and parenting books. To find your nearest library, go to:
www.gov.uk/local-library-services

### NCT

A charity for parents, providing antenatal and postnatal support and advice.

www.nct.org.uk

### The Reading Agency

This literacy charity runs creative programmes to help children's reading skills.

http://readingagency.org.uk/children/

### Schools admissions information

Government advice on finding out about local schools in your area.

www.gov.uk/schools-admissions/choosing-schools

### Sure Start Children's Centres

These centres provide early-learning and day-care centres for preschool children. To find your nearest centre, go to:

www.gov.uk/find-sure-start-childrens-centre

### What to Expect

Advice and information on pregnancy and parenting.

www.whattoexpect.com

## Medical information

### Bliss

A charity providing advice and support for premature and sick babies.

www.bliss.org.uk

### Great Ormond Street Hospital for Children website
General information and advice on children's health and medical issues.
www.gosh.nhs.uk

### KidsHealth
Information on children's health, behaviour and development.
http://kidshealth.org

### National Institute on Deafness and Other Communication Disorders (NIDCD)
Health information on deafness and hearing concerns.
www.nidcd.nih.gov

### NHS Choices
Information about conditions and treatments, as well as NHS services and support near you.
www.nhs.uk

### Public Health England Obesity
Information and research relating to obesity and weight concerns.
www.noo.org.uk

### Royal College of Psychiatrists: Postnatal depression advice
Information and a free downloadable leaflet on postnatal depression.
www.rcpsych.ac.uk/healthadvice/problemsdisorders/postnatal
depression.aspx

### WebMD
General information on specific conditions and treatments.
www.webmd.com

## Charities and special educational needs

### Blind Children UK
Advice and support for families of children with visual impairments.
www.blindchildrenuk.org

### Dyspraxia Foundation
Advice and support concerning dyspraxia, a form of developmental
coordination disorder.
www.dyspraxiafoundation.org.uk

### Go Kids Go!
A charity providing wheelchair skills training for children.
www.go-kids-go.org.uk

### Gov.uk information: children with special educational needs
Advice and resources for parents of children with special educational
needs that affect a child's ability to learn.
www.gov.uk/children-with-special-educational-needs/overview

### Mind
Information and support for mental health problems and concerns.
www.mind.org.uk

### The National Autistic Society
Information, support and services for people with autism (including
Asperger's syndrome) and their families.
www.autism.org.uk

### National Deaf Children's Society (NDCS)
Advice and support for deaf children and their families.
www.ndcs.org.uk

### Talking Point
Information and local services on speech and language development.
www.talkingpoint.org.uk

## Useful reading

Brown, David and Findlay, Arthur, *501 Days Out for Kids in the UK and Ireland* (Octopus Books, 2010)

David, Alison, *Help Your Child Love Reading* (Egmont, 2014)

Hughes Joshi, Liat, *New Old-Fashioned Parenting* (Summersdale Vie, 2015)

Hughes Joshi, Liat, *Raising Children: The Primary Years* (Pearson Prentice Hall Life, 2010)

Livingstone, Tessa, *Child of Our Time* (Bantam Press, 2005)

Sunderland, Margot, *The Science of Parenting* (DK, 2008)

# Acknowledgements

With thanks to Lucy Moody, Abby Wilkins and Sallie Floyed, who all contributed to make the book what it is (if you don't like it, blame one of them!); my mum, Sue Nicholas, for her attention; Sam Jackson at Ebury for her patience and persistence; the team at Fundamentally Children, who endured me stressing about this, the new website and the fact that there are only 24 hours in a day; and to Jack, for picking up the pieces.

# Index